Dear Peggy —

Lots of fond memories
of our "long" friendship

Love
Grace

My Adventures

by

Grace Black-Hammond

RoseDog✤Books
PITTSBURGH, PENNSYLVANIA 15222

The contents of this work including, but not limited to, the accuracy of events, people, and places depicted; opinions expressed; permission to use previously published materials included; and any advice given or actions advocated are solely the responsibility of the author, who assumes all liability for said work and indemnifies the publisher against any claims stemming from publication of the work.

RoseDog Books
701 Smithfield Street
Pittsburgh, PA 15222
Visit our website at *www.rosedogbookstore.com*

ISBN: 978-1-4809-9856-8
eISBN: 978-1-4809-9880-3

I would like to dedicate this story to all of the wonderful people who have helped me along the way-teachers, mentors, good friends and my husband of 51 years, James Black. My children; Karen, Susan, Barbara, Claire and John who have made me proud to be their mother. Also my grandchildren who have been a great joy to me. And last but not least my husband, Maury Hammond, who has helped me, put all of this on paper with great patience and encouragement.

Grace Black Hammond

Five generations: Karen, Ryan and Jada, Dad and Me

YOU SHOULD WRITE A BOOK

"You should write a book, Grace", so many people have said to me, so after many years of hesitation and procrastination, I decided that maybe my life story would be of interest to someone even if only my own family.

MOM AND DAD

I was born in 1931-a depression baby. My father, Earl Maze, was a guard at the Federal Reserve Bank in Pittsburgh. He was raised on a small farm in Washington, PA by his mother and stepfather. They were very poor. My grandmother was left with small children to raise after my grandfather was killed in a train accident. My Dad, the youngest, and his older brother, Harry, were sent to an orphanage until she could support them. They ran away, were retrieved by the police, returned to my grandmother and sent back to the orphanage. She finally married John Pratten-a hard drinking Irishman who had worked in the oilfields of PA hauling oil in wooden barrels with a wagon team. She then had a home for Dad & Harry. Dad joined the Marines when he was barely 17 and got to see some of the world aboard the airplane carrier, Saratoga,-that was in 1926. I have a photograph of Charles Lindbergh taken when he visited the carrier.

Charles Lindbergh visiting USS Saratoga, 1929

Dad used to laugh as he told the story of how he became a marine. He was walking down 5th Ave in Pittsburgh and stopped to look at a poster of a marine in dress uniform at a recruiting office. The officer in charge saw him and asked, "Would you like to be a marine, young man?" Dad replied, "Well I'm not yet old enough. I'm only 17." The recruiting officer said, "You can join if you have your parent's permission. Can we call your parents?" "Well my mother lives in the country and doesn't have a telephone at her house. She could be called at a neighbor's". The call was made and my grandmother said, "If Earl wants to join it's OK with me." Dad made the decision on the spot and was on his way to Paris Island that night!

Marine PFC and Corporal Earl Maze, 1928

My mother, Edith Roessler, was from another walk of life quite different from Dad's. She was from a rather well-to-do family and was raised wearing frilly lace dresses, fancy hats and button shoes. She was a "working girl" employed by the Federal Reserve Bank where she met Dad. Her family story was her father's lineage. He was the son of a very determined lady who was raised in the lap of luxury and was disinherited when she fell in love with and married the family's gardener. Had this not happened, Mom would have been a recipient of a large fortune. My dad always called them the "Blue Bloods"-such is life!

ENTER GRACE JANE

After a short romance, they eloped to West Virginia and kept the marriage a secret until I was conceived. They then moved in with my maternal grandmother until she passed away. They inherited a beautiful large house on the waterfront of the Ohio River in Pittsburgh. I was born in November, 1931, a chubby little girl with lots of dark hair and the apple of my Dad's eye. I don't remember much of life there except being told that I visited the neighbors every morning to have toast and jam. I guess I had the wanderlust even then. I was nearly killed running across the busy boulevard to greet my Dad coming home from work.

In order to keep the house they took in boarders: one couple and a widowed lady, Grace Jane, for whom I was named. I do remember her. She was very elegant, smoked a lot and snorted when she laughed. None of these people could pay any rent and consequently, the house was lost. These were hard times for everyone: the years 1931, 2 and 3.

When I was about 3 or 4, we moved to an apartment in Avalon on the third floor. I was rushed to the hospital at 4 years old for an emergency appendectomy and was quite proud of my scar. I caught the measles and was taken care of by our next-door neighbor while my brother, Bob, was brought home from the hospital. I could only see him through the entry door window. I remember I tried my new roller skates to the dismay of the people downstairs. We had an ice box that was cooled by a big chunk of ice which was delivered to the third floor.

What was it like growing up during this big economic crisis? I really can't say-we were never hungry for Dad always had work. My mother was a homebody although she still had many of her bank friends and always found time to play bridge. We did take vacations to Canandota Lake where I remember Dad trying to coax me to wade through the seaweed to swim further out-I just wouldn't do it and had to be carried out.

STARTING SCHOOL

I started school when we moved to a small house on Marie Ave. My best friend was a little black girl, Elva. We would comb the nearby woods picking wild flowers. We were inseparable. When I started school my Mom suggested tactfully that maybe I should make some 'other friends'. No reason why, only that it would be a good idea. I never forgot Elva even though we moved away shortly thereafter. She taught me a lot about us being equal in God's eyes.

Years later I met her in town and she introduced me to her husband-a huge very black man-I was surprised-I never thought of Elva as black.

First grade went well but we all lived in fear that we would get a certain 2nd grade teacher who was rumored to put you in a dark closet at the slightest infraction. When second grade started and I was assigned another teacher, I breathed a sigh of relief.

My mother's sister, Aunt Dottie and her husband visited us often-I didn't like him much and when he tried to bribe me for a kiss with an ice cream cone-I refused. I think I got the dripping cone anyway.

We moved to Bellevue when I started the 3rd grade. We lived on Grant Ave only 3 blocks from school. One day while we were having a Halloween party my little brother showed up. With all that candy he thought school was a pretty nice place. He returned so often the school had to call my mother to keep him home. We never did figure out what my mom was doing back then!

We moved to a new house on Dunbar Ave. It was a small 2 ½ bedroom house and 1 bath. We had a grand piano in the living room and it took up about 1/3 of the room. I remember Mom playing 'In the Garden' and learned to play the 'Marine Hymn'. Dad had his old uniform hanging downstairs and I helped him shine the buttons now and then

I had many happy years in grade school and was a good student. My memories of teachers were rather vague-an arithmetic teacher who had no compunction about using a ruler across your hands if she determined you weren't behaving. We were all scared to death of her but we all learned the multiplication tables very well!

Another teacher I will never forget was Miss Shoemaker. She taught English. She was the first and only teacher to give me a bad grade. I was so startled I never fooled around in her class again and to this day I cringe when I hear an improper verb.

Miss Shoemaker called me 'Grace'. Up until that time I was always called 'Grace Jane'. I went home and told my Mom and she said "Tell her your name is 'Grace Jane'. I did and her reply was, "I have 35 children in this class and it's all I can do to remember one name". I've been 'Grace' ever since. She took an interest in my poetry writing and was a real inspiration to me. I'll never forget her. She was there many years later at the funeral home when my mother died-telling me that all was still OK. I wrote a letter to her telling her how much she influenced my life.

During 5th grade I became an avid reader. One of my favorite books was "I Married Adventure" by Osa Johnson. It was a story of a small town girl who married a wildlife photographer and went with him to Africa. I thought that this must have been the most exciting life a person could have and I wanted to be just like her. The book had a brown and cream zebra printed cover. I never forgot Osa. I came in contact with her 2 other times in my future. I often daydreamed about going to faraway places. A great measure of my dreams came true!

The second time years later my daughter, Susan, and I traveled to Dallas. We were thinking about opening a shop and wanted to check out the Mart and gather information. We stopped for lunch in a small town and decided to walk across the way to an antique shop. While looking at old books, I spotted "I Married Adventure" by Osa Johnson, one of my childhood heroines. I had often thought back to those years and wondered what had become of her and if I could find that book-and there it was. I bought it and took it home to read again. It was just as fascinating as when I read it in the 5ᵗʰ grade.

I hurried home from school to listen to the radio a lot; 'Inner Sanctum', 'Stella Dallas' and 'Only the Shadow Knows'. If my parents went out, my brother and I would get into terrible fights about what to listen to. He wanted to listen to 'The Grand Ole Oprey' and I hated that music. I preferred popular music. Today he can't stand country music and I love it!

Our next door neighbors were the Dredges. Mrs D was a faith healer. My Dad was very skeptical of her claims until one day he was home from work suffering from a terrible headache that didn't respond to aspirin and he was about to call the doctor. My mother called on Mrs Dredge and she told Dad to lie down on the sofa and she would pray for him. He reluctantly complied. He then fell asleep and awoke without the headache. This made a believer out of him and all of us too! Years later after Mrs Dredge's death a small trunk in her attic revealed many letters from those she had helped. Are there really people who have this gift? My explanation and reading later about Edward Casey has convinced me there are. The Dredges had a son, Vic, who came home to live for awhile after the war. He was a handsome man and very friendly to my brother and me. We kept track of him for many years. The whole family made a deep impression on me.

I didn't get too many spankings when I was growing up-in fact, I can only remember one. I was always very curious of my Dad's gun which he thought was well hidden in the chifforobe locked up, but the key was on top. It didn't take me long to find my way into the gun case, take it out and look at it. He never knew about that. I loved to go with him to shooting practice. He was an expert marksman in pistol shooting & had many awards. One day he was going shooting and said I couldn't go along so I climbed onto the running board of the car as he was pulling away. He got out of the car and I ran up 3 flights of stairs and hid under the bed. When he caught up with me he said, "Come out of there" and meekly I did-hence a pretty good spanking occurred. The gig was up and I realized I might as well take my punishment or spend the rest of my life under the bed. I was usually a very quiet child and they always said of me "Still waters run deep"! I guess I was always Daddy's girl. I have so many fond memories of him buying rabbit fur mittens and bringing home Shirley Temple dresses when we probably couldn't afford them.

All during my early childhood I usually walked every Sunday to Sunday school at the Green Stone Methodist Church-about ¾ mile away. Dad and I were baptized together there when I was 5 years old. Many times our family doctor taking his daughter to the same church stopped to give me a ride. I continued on at that church until my brother who had a beautiful soprano voice started singing at the Baptist church. A neighbor of ours who attended that church took an interest in him and consequently we all got involved in the Baptist church. There I was very influenced by the minister, Bert Jackstiet, and stayed on until I married and left for Venezuela. I was always a big admirer of Billy Graham who started touring the country in a program called Youth for Christ.

GRANDMA'S HOUSE

We almost always went to Grandma's house on Saturday or Sunday. Her name was Lydia Jane. She had chicken and home-made noodles waiting for us. My daughter, Karen, although very young when we visited her always called her the 'Grandma with the noodles on the bed'. She had her noodles laid out drying on a paper on the bed and that was a pretty unusual sight for a three-year-old. I, on the other hand, when visiting the farm was afraid of every moving thing-"Watch out for that duck-he'll snap at you; and that one rooster is pretty mean. Don't get too close to the edge of the pig pen, the mother pig could hurt you". My job was to go through the pasture to the spring house to get the butter. As I walked there all of the cows stared at me with very scary eyes and I usually broke into a run for fear I was about to be attacked. Still, these outings were always enjoyable and sometime Grandpa Pratten would break into a dance he called the 'Big Apple'.

One terrifying experience that I'll probably never forget was watching Grandma milking a cow and SPLAT all over me. After washing me down I remember saying "If she does that again you'll give her a good kick, won't you, Grandma?" She assured me she definitely would and I was satisfied that the cow would get her proper punishment. Is this what caused my freckles?

My grandmother is one of my heros. For the last 12 years of her life she was legally blind and deaf. She always had a hearty laugh and somehow recognized us when we came to visit. We always got a birthday card from her when we were growing up and she could tell you your age and birth date as long as she lived.

She had a hard life having been left a widow with 8 children 5 still at home. She went to work in a glass factory, nursed the sick and prepared bodies for burial. She was a good Christian woman. She thought Oral Roberts hung the moon. She was there when I came home for my mother's funeral-a pillar of strength. The last time I saw her she said she was just waiting for the angels to take her home. They came in her sleep when she was 104 years old. To this day I keep her in my heart and know there isn't anything I can't get through 'cause Grandma got through just about every tragedy in life and still had her ready laugh while telling us stories of her past. Grandpa Pratten said he knew her family history and she was one quarter Indian. She never acknowledged that part except once at the dinner table when we were trying to get her to say one way or another about the story she looked up and said, "How".

Grandpa Pratten was the only grandfather I knew and he was quite a case. We used to look on in awe when he ate peas by his lining them up on a knife. He always broke up bread and put it in his coffee with a little whiskey, if available. He and Grandma had one son, Wilbert, and he was very proud of him. He had an Irishman's yen for drink but Grandma was able to keep him in control most of the time. One time we arrived for our usual Sunday visit and found him with a black eye. The story came out finally that it was due to a heavy country coffee cup being thrown across the table. He was very contrite that day and Grandma never admitted the deed!

All in all I had a pretty happy childhood. My Mom and Dad took in a little boy, Tommy, 15 months old from The Children's Aid Society and he stayed with us until he became 5 years old at which time his birth mother insisted he be raised Catholic. Even though my Mom and Dad agreed to send him to the Catholic Church, they refused so they came and took him away. We never heard from him again. A very sad day for all of us.

That summer I broke my arm riding on the handle bars of my friend's bicycle.

The next summer we spent several weeks in Washington, PA with relatives while my Mom and Dad went to Philadelphia for a job training program. We spent many days picking black berries to sell and ate plenty of them. I later found out that blackberry bushes were a favorite place for rattlesnakes. We went blithely about our picking and never saw one. I think we sold them for 5 cents a pint. We listened on the radio to our cousin who sang and played country music. We thought we were surely related to a big celebrity! Dad and Mom came home and Dad went to the hospital with stomach ulcers. Shortly after he joined the Jewel Tea Company and became one of their top salesmen.

Our house had a terrace of roses and honeysuckles on the porch-peonies and lilacs in the back yard. Growing up in those days was not much like it is today- no I-pads, no texting- just playing outside till dark-hopscotch, 'Mother, May I', riding bikes, walking pretty long distances to the local swimming pool-picking violets on the hill. Usually I got money to go to the movies on Saturday when the Frankenstein movies came out. We had serials that continued for a month or so and you could hardly wait for the next one. We sometimes went to the late show then ran most of the way home after the lights on Main St turned off especially when we passed the 'big stone house' that we were sure was haunted. I remember the trees swaying in the shadows and imagined all sorts of ghosts and goblins hiding behind the bushes. I had a job going to the grocery store for a neighbor and got 10 cents for a walk to Main St about ½ mile each way. I collected grease and tin foil for the war effort.

THE TERRIBLE TEENS WEREN'T SO BAD

When I was 13 I received an art scholarship to Carnegie Tech and started going to classes on Saturdays. It became too much trouble to travel by bus or street car to get to downtown Pittsburgh, transfer to a street car to get to Carnegie, so I finally gave up though it was a great opportunity for a girl my age.

By the time I started high school we still lived on Dunbar Ave. It was about ½ mile from school and we walked to school and home for lunch. My children always tease me saying, "Oh yes, Mom, we know it was uphill all the way and knee deep in snow". Not really; it was uphill only half way and the snow was only ankle deep! I remember fighting with my Mom to let me wear ankle socks instead of knee socks. I think I won that argument or at least folded the knee socks down to look like anklets!

FRANK SINATRA!

I was right at the age when the rage over Frank Sinatra was at its height. He was coming to town! My mom agreed to allow me and my friend, Martha Jean from across the street to go into Pittsburgh to see the show. It was at the Stanley Theater. The way the show was scheduled it would appear after the movie was over then the same show was repeated and again another performance. We paid our admission and sat through the movie anxiously waiting for Frankie. When he did come on, the place went wild-girls were swooning all over the place and each time he did a little curl of his lip, out came another round of screams. Well, I didn't swoon or scream but I thought he was wonderful. We stayed and watched the movie again and saw him perform a second time.

We arrived home much later than we were expected and both of us were steadfast fans of Frankie's for the rest of his life. It always amazed me that he became a talented dancer and actor-he was truly an exceptional entertainer! The song, That Old Black Magic was That Old Sinatra Magic.

High School was a new kettle of fish. The clique from the other grade school arrived and they were all very popular and exclusive in their choice of new friends. Our school had sororities and fraternities and I wasn't pledged my first year. I was devastated. I had always found it easy to make friends although I was rather shy. This to a teen-ager was so important. My sophomore year I joined a sorority called the Hegadophs. I can't even remember what that stood for but we had a lot of good times together and I made many new friends. We took a trip to Lake Erie and had all sorts of activities. Most of my friends were older than me. I was elected Secretary and then President.

I was a good student. My special interest was the chorus and I sang for 4 years. We once even traveled to the state prison to give a concert. However, my business math teacher, Mrs Riener wrote in my album, "To Grace who thinks of other things than math".

I usually paid a weekly visit to my aunt Ethyl. She was a very "regal" lady, sickly, always sat in a lounge chair with a beautiful cover over her legs. She was soft spoken and seemed genuinely interested in the tales of a young girl. We spent many afternoons having tea and talking. I really admired her and hoped some day to be just like her. I didn't quite make it but she also was one of my heroes!

In high school I opted for the business curriculum; shorthand, typing and business math along with the other usual studies. I sailed through most of my studies except algebra. I got through that by the skin of my teeth.

When I was barely 15 I started working at Rosenbaum Department Store as an "extra" Monday nights and Saturdays. I worked in just about every department even the mailing room. There I made extra money and became interested in dress design. My Mom made most of my clothes and I bought the material. Our family didn't have much money in those days. I remember Mom sewing away on an old treadle machine and making me some very nice prom dresses of my own design. I got a raise in wages when the minimum wage was raised to 75 cents an hour! Before my senior year I became a paid employee of Lancome Perfume Company at the store.

I had a high school boy friend who owned a car. That was very unusual at the time and it was about the only car at school. He was a junior and I was a freshman. My interest in him flew out the window when I met my future husband, a junior at the U of Pittsburgh on a blind date. My friend, Nancy Smith, had a second cousin, Roy Gass, that she dated occasionally and he had this friend-would I like to double date with him? He and Roy arrived at her house and we were very excited-"a big college guy". Nancy's mother greeted them at the door while we were getting dressed. She came in with the assessment-"What's he look like" we asked- "Well" she said, "He's tall". He was a mechanical engineering student and an Air Force vet-WOW! We fell for each other almost immediately and went together till he graduated from college and I from high school. That was in 1949. His name was Jim Black. One year later I became Mrs Black and we were married 51 years.

Jim's family, the Blacks, were from Greensboro, PA, a farm community 60 miles south of Pittsburgh on the border of West Virginia. The main claim to fame there was his grandmother's family, the Hamiltons who had a pottery factory. Later the pottery became collectors items. Old pots that the kids used to use for target practice are now selling for $250. The Blacks were early founders of the town

Through-out all my high school years I remember looking at ads in the employment pages for far away places. They were usually to sell magazines in some other state. Not quite what I was looking for. Jim's ambition was to go to South Africa-that sounded pretty wonderful to me. He finally interviewed with Gulf Oil and accepted a job in Venezuela. It was a 2 year assignment. He bought me an engagement ring with money he borrowed from his sister and promised me he would return as soon as possible. I can't say I was too happy with this idea but decided he was worth waiting for-besides a chance to travel had always been my dream. Little did I know I would spend the next 35 years in 9 countries!

MY SHORT-LIVED CAREER AS A WORKING GIRL

I took a job with a hardware store supposedly in the business department. That wasn't quite what they wanted; they needed someone for sales too. I was elected to do both. Hardware wasn't my forte but I made a valiant effort to learn the "nuts and bolts" of the business. It worked out pretty well until, needing help with a customer, I happened on the owner and the business manager in a compromising position upstairs behind some packing boxes. WHOA-this was a situation I wasn't prepared for. I pretended I didn't know what was going on but things got a little strained around there.

At this point I heard from Jim (We wrote almost every day) that he could get 10 days off at Christmas time and could come to Florida to his sister's house. My employment ended by mutual consent when I announced that I needed 2 weeks off for Christmas. We made arrangements to meet in Florida and Mrs Black would accompany me. My parents weren't too thrilled with the idea but finally gave in to their strong-willed daughter. We had a wonderful reunion. Jim headed back to Venezuela saying he was pretty sure that Gulf would allow him to marry and provide housing before his 2 years were up although it was highly unusual.

I went back to Pittsburgh and got a job with Graybar Electric Company in the accounts payable department. See, Mrs Reiner, I was listening in class! It was a great job. We dashed into the lunch room, gulped down lunch and played "500" till start-up time. I was really enjoying it and beginning to think I might like being a career girl!

I started making plans for a July wedding as Jim said he could come home for 3 weeks. I spent every penny I had saved so I could have a perfect wedding.

THE BIG DAY

My best friend, Peggy Dolan, and I went out to the U of Pittsburgh to see the Dean of Women to petition for a wedding at Heinz Memorial Chapel. It was a daunting experience for an 18 year old girl who just graduated from high school to enter the great tower of learning and ask for the chapel. It turned out to be very easy; the Dean was very nice and helpful and we came away with a date; July 29, 1950.

Heinz Chapel was a beautiful place, stained glass windows so beautiful they took your breath away, gothic architecture and the longest aisle in the city of Pittsburgh. That was the first step in my big plan.

I ordered and paid for my own dress, a beautiful organdy lace dress I saw in a magazine. I made my own veil and the bridesmaids' hats, set up the Schenley Hotel for the reception and ordered the flowers. Now all I needed was for the groom to show up!

The next month passed slowly and Jim arrived as scheduled. Nancy would be Maid of Honor. Peggy Dolan, one of my best friends and Jim's sister, Jean, were bridesmaids. Jim lined up his cousin, George Gabler, my brother and his childhood best friend, George Williamson. A high school friend was to sing 'Ave Maria, 'Because' and the 'Lord's Prayer'. The bridesmaids were dressed in organdy, apple green and lavender carrying daisies and yellow roses. The men were all in white jackets and Jim looked very handsome. I carried a white bible and white orchids.

All came off without a hitch. The deed was done and I had a wedding every girl dreams about. The reception at the Schenley had to be liquor free because the family matriarch, Aunt Asia, was a member of Women's Christian Temperance Union. An old family friend played the piano.

July 29, 1950

During the reception the groom and his dad disappeared and I couldn't imagine where they could be. A mutual friend said, "I think Mr Black has a bottle of whiskey and they went up to have a little nip"! I wasn't too happy but what could I do except express my dislike with a look of dissatisfaction and a few "wifely words' when they returned?

After the reception we all went back to my parent's home where Jim's mom sighed and told my aunt, "He's so young-just 23". To which my aunt said, "Well, she's just 18". That was the first time Jim's family knew my age. Jim didn't let them in on that little bit of information. I guess he thought they might think he robbed the cradle-which he did!

GOODBYE PENNSYLVANIA

We left for our honeymoon-I in my own designed dress of apple green silk and a straw hat with roses. We were off to the Summit Hotel in West Virginia. On our way we got a ticket for one-arm driving. What a KILLJOY that police officer was. The next day we stopped off in Greensboro at the Blacks so all the relatives there could get a chance to meet the new bride. Then back to Pittsburgh to pack up my luggage and from there to the train station for New York where we would board the Santa Paula Grace Line ship to Caracas, Venezuela.

While in New York we went to a French Restaurant that Mrs Black had gone to years ago. We asked a taxi driver if he knew it and he said, "Yes". It was just around the corner. We had filet mignon and cherries jubilee, a desert with spun sugar so wonderful I've been looking for it since; I've never found anything comparable. We saw all of the sights we could in 2 days. Jim had to stop in the Gulf office and we were on our way!

THE HONEYMOON SHIP

The Santa Paula was one of Grace Line's largest ships. It was a wonderful trip a real eye-opener for a small town girl! We met several young honeymooners who were from New York wealthy families and each one had a larger diamond than the last. We stopped off in Curacao and then on to Caracas where we stayed at the Tomanaco Hotel waiting for our flight the next day to the San Tome oil camp.

THE BEAUTIFUL TROPICS

"San Tome", Eastern Venezuela was the land of swaying palm trees and gardenias growing on the bushes by the houses.

In Venezuela

Oh, palm trees wave and flowers bloom
        In Venezuela!
The jasmine sheds its sweet perfume
        In Venezuela!
The poinsettias gorgeous flare,
        The roses, lilies, orchids rare,
In gay profusion everywhere,
        In Venezuela!
Oh, mountains lift their heads up high
        In Venezuela!
And wondrous sunsets tint the sky

In Venezuela!
The silver rivers glide along,
While hidden birds pour forth their song
And forests dense with shy life throng
        In Venezuela!

What if wealth lies 'neath the soil,
        In Venezuela?
"Manana" is the day of toil
        In Venezuela!
In evening cool while soft moon beams,
Soft music floats and dark eye gleams,
Ah, surely, "tis a land of dreams,
        This Venezuela!

Author unknown

I was full of expectations-finally I was realizing my day dreams and couldn't wait to see the swaying palms and beautiful country that was to be my future home. We finally boarded the 'Gulf' plane to take us to San Tome. It was a cargo plane, seats aligned horizontally on each side. I expected to be issued a parachute! It was a prop plane (all were prop in those days) and it took us forever. The door opened and I was greeted by 25 or so men all dressed in khaki lined up at attention to get a look at the new bride. They all tried to speak only Spanish but that didn't last too long as their vocabularies were pretty limited. Well, I passed that test-on to my new home. Oh yes, there were 2 palm trees and the air terminal was a tin shack. Something was wrong with this picture and I began wondering what I had gotten myself into!

The araguaney, Venezuela's national tree

MY NEW HOME, CAMP #1

We made our way to our new home-2 rooms, a cement floor, tin roof and the door and window trim were painted in Gulf orange. No air conditioning but the weather seemed very pleasant. The kitchen was furnished with great care by Jim's bachelor friends with cookware borrowed from the mess hall-pots and pans large enough to cook for 50.

First house in Venezuela and old road from Caracas to airport

Three of Jim's friends came in as soon as we arrived and brought cold beer. They stayed on and on. We finally got rid of them, unpacked a little and fell into bed-which, of course, they had short sheeted! Jim assured me we wouldn't be staying there long-maybe only a year and we might be able to get a vacation house (someone going to the States for vacation). They say that love is blind but this was stretching it a little!

I don't remember too much about those first few weeks except it was HOT! Our first social occasion was a Department BBQ at the river. We met a lot of nice people all trying to HELP. There was even a local frog calling, "HELP" in the distance. I arrived home with so many mosquito bites I couldn't count them-I gave up at 50 on one leg. The only good thing about that experience was that for many years I was immune to mosquito bites.

THE NEW COOK

We had a commissary to buy groceries. Not quite Stateside but we managed. One of my first meals was chili. No chili powder so I substituted jalapenos which I had never seen before-not exactly a Pittsburgh staple. After nearly blinding myself from rubbing my eye after chopping them, I tasted the chili and it was so hot we couldn't eat it. I finally added a lot more tomato sauce and finally got it down followed by a lot of water.

My culinary talents were sadly lacking. My only original dish was corn fritters that I made at Home Ec class. I couldn't call Mom for help so Jim had to suffer a lot.

Our small shipment finally arrived with the bare necessities. I tried to dress up the little place which was furnished with metal chests of drawers and head boards, one bamboo sofa and chair, a dining table of formica and 2 wooden chairs. I made curtains from some local material and had 2 small throw rugs. I guess starting out with cement floors and no rugs ruined me forever. For many years I couldn't get enough rugs.

FRIENDS

There were several other newly married couples that arrived at the same time and we became fast friends. Our next door neighbors were Rose and Bernie Texeira from British Guiana. Rose became my best friend and remained so till her death in 2008. Our houses were back-to-back and Bernie always sang in the shower-I in my own shower sometimes joined in. Bernie always joked that we sang in the shower together.

LIFE IN THE FAST LANE!?

Most of Jim's best friends were bachelors and we all had a great time. We had a movie a week and a club house. That was it, so we pretty much had to entertain ourselves. We had 'break-up-the-week' parties on Wednesdays and there was always something going on on weekends.

I had never had anything to drink before and so this was pretty new to me. Everyone else was older and much more experienced in just about everything. My foray into drinking was the offer of a salty dog which tasted pretty good, but after a couple left me with a swirling head, leaving the party early and spending the night in the bathroom, I haven't had one since!

Many of the bachelors were dating the nurses, school teachers and secretaries that came in from the states. They were all thoroughly scrutinized at the PR Department by the men, and their employment applications were combed over well in advance of their arrival. When they stepped off the plane they were surrounded by eager guys who tried to look like the man of their dreams. Many of the women ended up marrying these eager bachelors and lived happily ever after.

At that time all nurses, school teachers and secretaries were Americans or Brits. Eventually local women were hired and that was probably the first time women from Venezuelan families ever worked out of their home in a real job for the oil companies. Consequently, they pretty much all married American men. One family with 4 beautiful daughters saw them snatched up immediately. The only people my age were college 'kids' who came in for the summer to be with their families. I considered them 'kids'. Many years later I met one of them and found out we were the same age! Gulf oil had a hospital with Venezuelan doctors who had trained and studied in the States and American nurses. The hospital was run pretty well but it was on a first come-first served basis and sometimes there were long waits in the halls for your turn. They served all US and Venezuelan personnel so it was pretty crowded most of the time (a small taste of socialized medicine).

We had 2 camps; North and South. Most of the Venezuelan oil workers lived in South Camp and the expats, Venezuelan doctors, engineers, etc lived in North Camp.

The permanent houses were pretty much the same; some a little larger and, of course, the Department heads had the nice ones.

The contracts were for 2 years and then a 2-month vacation, so we were prepared for a long stay.

The commissary was well stocked with imported foods-frozen milk, some vegetables and eggs and very little meat. Often we went out and bought a beef from a local rancher and had it butchered at the commissary. It was pretty bad and often we could only use it for ground meat. You could stop in at the South Camp open market for tenderloin if you overlooked the flies buzzing around the meat that was hanging in the open. We took it home, marinated it and grilled it. A Spanish couple raised chickens so we bought chicken and eggs from them. When we went back to the States we could hardly believe there were whole rows of just cereal!

We had a club that showed a movie a week and they eventually added a pool and snack bar. None of the women had cars so we walked or rode bicycles to the pool. The men were issued pickups or coupes-all "Gulf Orange". The bachelors had a mess hall that served family style. We ate there once in a while and the food was pretty good; probably better than my cooking. I remember one guy coming in after too many drinks at the club and having a dish of jalapenos which he thought was OKRA. The others let him gulp down a spoonful and he ran out choking and gagging. The others thought it was hilariously funny-a sort of sadistic humor that sometimes took hold when there was nothing better to do.

There was one restaurant about a mile away in Tigrito; 'Chepas'. It was run by a Venezuelan lady. Some Texan taught her to do steak and gravy with mashed potatoes. I don't know where she got her steak but it was pretty good. Desert was flan or casco de guavas with saltine crackers and cream cheese. It was a favorite spot for 'dinner out on the town'. On the road there were Venezuelan women doing their wash in the river.

Some weekends we investigated nearby streams for fishing. One of my first trips to the river for fishing was pretty much a disaster. We went with another couple just for a day trip. We were all aware that most of the streams were filled with piranhas - a very dangerous man-eating fish so we were being very careful. The 2 men went ahead up stream and I and the other gal were making our way along a steep slippery bank. Suddenly my foot slipped and I fell in the water-splashing and screaming in fear of being eaten alive. A yell from upstream came, "Be quiet down there. You're scaring the fish away!" Right then I discovered where I stood in relation to fishing's importance.

On a short weekend vacation we drove to Maturin with Jim's buddy, Charlie Wheeler. He and Jim had a running argument on just about everything especially politics. They really enjoyed the 'art of discussion'. I listened to many arguments-some the same as last week's-Jim a liberal and Charlie a conservative. Jim finally became a conservative and years later while visiting Charlie in Texas they could hardly think of anything to say to each other. Jim eventually said, "If you are young and aren't liberal, you have no heart- when you mature and aren't a conservative, you have no brain". Charlie passed away in his sleep unexpectedly several months after Jim died and I always thought he just couldn't stand the idea of Jim getting up to the pearly gates and only telling his side of the story

Jim came down with strep throat and the doctors decided he would need his tonsils removed. He was hospitalized and they did the operation the old fashioned way-'pulled them out' with local anesthesia. It wasn't a good experience.

While he was hospitalized I bought a Pekinese puppy. I took it to the hospital window so Jim could see it from his room. He would have said, "Take it back", but since he couldn't talk, PANCHO became a member of our family; 'Like it or lump it'. As it turned out he pretty much lumped it as PANCHO didn't like Jim at all. He barely tolerated his presence. Pancho was a fighter and we had to rescue him many times from a fight with a much bigger dog. We nearly lost him many times. Finally we were to go on vacation and a friend kept him. They spoiled him so much he kept going back to see them and we decided to let them keep him; he found a home with '2 loving parents'.

BABY TIME

I was expecting our first baby in 1951 and decided to go to the States. My friend, Rose, said, "Bring me back a blue-eyed blond". I replied, "Not much chance of that" with Jim and I dark haired and brown eyed. She thought she was making a joke! I was 7 months pregnant. Jim put me on a plane in San Tome for Caracas where I had to make a change for New York and on to Pittsburgh. That turned out to be a traumatic experience. The plane went out on the runway 3 times and they finally decided it was a 'no go'. Each time we loaded and unloaded I had to wait about 2 hours. During one of these waits I went into the bathroom and cried my eyes out. We were transported to La Guira for the night, picked up the next morning and boarded the same plane. I was never so glad to get to the USA. A change in New York and into the waiting arms of my Mom and Dad!

Jim followed 6 weeks later and Karen Louise was born on schedule. 9 1/2 pounds-22 ½ inches long. WHAT?!- she had blue eyes. It was a long labor and the doctor told Jim to go home and wait. He promptly went home and went to sleep. He had the reputation of being able to sleep anywhere and anytime. My Dad kept calling the hospital every hour on the hour. Jim came in shortly handing out cigars and announced he was leaving the next day for Greensboro to go deer hunting with his uncle. He tried to convince me I was in the best of hands. Something was wrong with this picture and I wasn't too pleased, I don't think he was ready to be a father; after all, he was only 25!? Who was this little stranger crying in the night? Of course, I wasn't "quite ready" either-I was only 20. I managed quite nicely though. The doctor said she should eat every 4 hours and I tried to wake her-she really just wanted to sleep. She was her father's daughter! By the way, the hunting trip was cancelled!

As soon as I was able to travel we made our way back to Venezuela via Orlando where Karen Louise was baptized with her paternal grandparents and Jim's sister and brother-in-law in attendance.

Baby Karen had a lot of attention from admiring friends. Her hair started coming in and it was blond. We thought her eyes would change color but they remained blue. When Rose saw her she said, "Well, I see I got my order". She was quite a contrast to Rose's new baby, Mario, who had curly brown hair and big beautiful brown eyes.

WOW-WE HAD A MAID!

One of the good?? things about living in a third world country was having household help. The first one I hired was a Trinidadian and she had a friend who hired on as gardener. I couldn't speak Spanish so I thought this was ideal. The only trouble was their English was 'Island English' and almost impossible to understand. We managed with a lot of sign language and got on fairly well. I had a big pork roast from the commissary and after our dinner while cleaning up I told the maid she could have some for dinner. She left for home and when I looked in the refrigerator the huge leftover roast was gone only the bone was left. The next day I asked what happened to it and she said, "I ate it ma'am". I guess it was the best meal she had in a long time. So often with most of the help it wasn't unusual that they had never seen most of what we took for granted; like a toilet or hot water in the sink. It was a learning experience for everyone. Many times the many things we had were too much of a temptation and I'm sure they thought we wouldn't miss a few things. We quite often had to explain that one shouldn't just take things-just ask for what they needed and if we could we would give them what they asked for. This usually worked out well and everyone was happy. Sometimes it was like taking a child to raise; everything had to be explained in detail. One day while I was ironing khaki pants and shirts which all the men wore to work there came a knock on the door; a woman asking for work. I said, "Can you iron khakis"? She said, "Yes, ma'am". I hired her on the spot and I never ironed khakis again.

FINALLY A REAL HOUSE

Life in Venezuela seemed just about perfect. We got a permanent H TYPE; meaning kitchen and dining room on one side, a living room in the middle and 2 bedrooms on the other side. We had a big patio with a mango tree growing in the middle and, yes, finally a palm tree and a gardenia bush!

THE LITTLE HOUSE OF HORRORS

Our dream house turned out to be a nightmare. We were infested with roaches. We tried everything to get rid of them. The house had an air space above the particle board ceiling and they came down from hiding day and night. I got very good at killing roaches but to this day my skin crawls at the sight of one. They got so bad that we called in the Company exterminators. I was about to go crazy. One night I awoke to a crunching noise and there on the dresser were about 10 roaches nibbling away at my imitation leather jewelry box. The next night I had a nightmare that one was in bed with us- screamed and jumped out of bed. Scared Jim to death but when I turned back the sheets-sure enough-there it was. We finally moved from that house to a new house by the golf course-just in time before I became a raving maniac.

NEW HOUSE NEW BABY

That next year, 1953, Susan Elizabeth was born. We now had 2 beautiful little girls. Our good friends, The Wheelers had their first baby about the same time and they named her Elizabeth Susan. Our Susan had brown eyes and brown hair and lots of it. We had many friends. We were all pretty much in the same boat. Our friends became our family since we were all so far from home.

Peggy Wheeler was from PA too so we became good friends. She came to Venezuela as a nurse and stayed on when she and Charlie decided to marry. Peggy and I were 6 months pregnant and went on a wild ride to Caracas together to the only good dentist available. After a couple of days there we were to go back down the treacherous road to the airport. We decided on a local bus-BAD IDEA. The bus was filled with Venezuelans, pots and pans and live chickens and 2 very scared Americans holding on for their lives as the driver made his way down the steep dirt road without a care in the world talking to passengers, laughing and having a wonderful ride, oblivious of sharp turns, narrow places and the 2 very silent women with white knuckles and clenched teeth! We made it back to San Tome wondering if we had caused permanent damage to our unborn babies.

Life in an oil camp was quite different than back home but everyone made the best of what was there keeping in mind all of the good things and overlooking the bad. The friends we made were lasting ones. I think we were a good influence on the locals; providing jobs, education, and a look into what a better life could be with hard work and perseverance.

These years, 17 in all, were some of the best years of my life. Jim was doing well in his work. We had a nice house, 2 darling little girls and lots of friends.

A NEW KID ON THE BLOCK

Barbara Jean was born December 18, 1954, at the San Tome hospital. Her birth was a little different than the others. I was home with the 2 little ones and I felt labor coming on. I called Jim at the club and said, 'I think I'm ready". He arrived shortly and we hurried to the hospital. The nurse said, "The doctor's on the way". Barbara was born in the hospital hallway on the way to the delivery room. She was a chubby, delightful baby and in a hurry to join her 2 sisters in the Black bevy of girls. She has never been early for anything since.

OFF TO ANACO

Shortly after Barbara was born we were transferred to Anaco an oil camp about 30 miles away. We weren't too happy to move but Father Gulf said, "Go" and we went. We lived in this Gulf camp until 1957. To complicate matters I was expecting again. One of our friends offered the use of their house in San Tome while they went on vacation. I stayed there awaiting the birth of the baby and Jim travelled back and forth.

THE JAIL BIRD

One evening while waiting for Jim to get home a call came. It was Jim calling from the police station. The road police stopped him and said he was speeding which he wasn't. He was so upset he argued the point and off he went to jail! "Grace, help, call someone and see if they can get me out of this place". Finally after a lot of negotiation and a few Bolivars (money) he was freed with the promise to appear in court to plead his case. He went with Senor Caballos, all was settled and he learned to say, "Si, Senor" and "No Senor" to any and all law enforcement.

TRAGEDY STRIKES HOME

On May 30, 1956, James Alexander Black III was born, 9 lbs 8 oz, our first boy. Jim was elated and we were all set to have a 4th little one in our family. After 7 days I brought the new little guy home to the anxiously awaiting little sisters. He lived only a week. I noticed he wasn't breathing as he should and we took him immediately to the hospital. It was a staph infection from the hospital. The next week was a flurry of unbelief and sadness. The whole community was there to help us get through this tragedy and our first born son was buried in a small graveyard close to San Tome.

MY SON

Far away in another land,
Lies a little part of me.
In a very small grave untouched by hand,
With no flowers there to see,

The flowers that cover and the thoughts that care,
Can only be found in my heart somewhere.
But somehow I feel when the spring flowers bloom,
Or the sun sets quietly and alone in my room,
Or when the others still sleep at the break of day,
He's here with me and he likes it this way.

I was brokenhearted but had 3 little girls to care for and although I was very depressed, visions of my grandmother came to mind and I hoped I had some of her fortitude in my genes to withstand this tragedy. I made it through it all and we went back to Anaco to start life again.

We travelled back and forth to San Tome to visit our friends there. Peggy Wheeler came down with a kidney infection and had to be hospitalized so I packed up my girls and went to take care of their 3 little ones. While getting them all down for a nap my Barbara climbed onto my lap and said, "Momma, you're so comfortable" and for no reason I started crying-I felt a terrible sadness. The next morning Charlie came in with a telegram that my mother had passed away.

I traveled to the US leaving my 3 with friends for my mother's funeral. Grandma was a pillar of strength for all of us. Mom was only 52 and my Dad was 49. Home was never home again and I finally realized my own home was the only home I had left.

AN AMERICAN IN CANTAURA
ON OUR OWN
THE HOUSE OF MANY COLORS

About that time Jim started talking about going into business with a good friend, a Venezuelan, Arturo Caballos. It meant leaving the protective wings of Father Gulf. We finally decided to cash in our insurance policies, all our savings and take the plunge. It meant finding a place to live on our own which wasn't easy at that time. Caballos said he could find us a place in Cantaura, a town nearby. We went and looked at it and it wasn't too bad. Each room had every wall painted a different color, cement floors and a huge cistern on top of the house to hold water. Not quite what we were used to but livable. We gathered up all our savings, located a few investors and Caballos dug up his FONDO (gold coins). He and Jim went to the bank, got a certified check and Jim went off to Dallas to buy a workover rig. When he returned he brought his Mom & Dad with him and we all moved into our "House of Many Colors.

SCHOOL DAYS

Karen and Susan went to the local Nun's school. We brought them the proper uniforms, blue skirt, white shirt and blue tie. The local kids teased them unmercifully calling Karen the Blue Eyed Yankee. She was the only one in school with blue eyes and blond hair. Karen managed to stick it out. Susan, however was more tenderhearted and came home crying and started bed wetting, so since it was only pre-kindergarten we kept her home. Karen dressed in her blue and white uniform went off determinedly every day and she finally convinced the Venezuelan kids that a blue eyed Yankee wasn't too bad after all!

I had planned a birthday party for Karen and invited some of the Venezuelan children. All was ready, piñata, cake and ice cream; little did I know the Venezuelan custom that the whole family would attend. Luckily, I had a big cake and cup cakes and Jim rushed out for more ice cream.

REVOLUTION

While we were living in Cantaura the government fell. Perez Jimendez left the country and all was in turmoil. There came a knock on our door in the middle of the night. It was Perucho, Cababallos' chauffeur/right hand man. He said Caballos wanted us to leave town with his car and ours and go to San Tome for safety. It was uncertain what had happened to him as the 'People' were on the rampage and had already killed several city mayors. We bundled up the 3 girls and took a few clothes, Jim driving the Caballos' car and me the family car and high tailed it out of town in hopes we wouldn't be stopped along the way. We met the Chief of Police and he was on the way out too. We never saw him again. We made it to San Tome 30 miles away, knocked on the Wheeler's door and they took us in for a week. When we returned to Cantaura everything had calmed down. Caballos was safe although he had spent 2 days locked up in jail. The people of the town liked him as he had a reputation of being a fair, kind man.

Revolution is a way of life in many South American countries. I only wish they had thrown Hugo Chavez out on his ear.

NALCO CAMP OUR HOME FOR 10 YEARS

We got wind of a new housing development in Anaco and it was soon to be finished so we decided to rent one of the houses. It was in Nalco Camp. I was expecting again and we moved in when Claire Elaine was 1 month old.

She was born on New Year's eve. Jim came to the hospital and announced he would be baby sitting the Wheeler kids so Peggy and Charlie could go to the party. The nurse woke me up early the next morning and told me, "I saw your husband at the party last night handing out cigars and having a great time". Seems they found another baby sitter.

I sure felt put upon spending New Year's Eve, 1958, in the hospital but Claire Elaine made up for it 100 fold!

Jim's Mom and Dad were a big help when we moved to Nalco as soon as the house was finished. We lived there 10 years. We made many trips to the beautiful beach at Puerta La Cruz-Silver Island where the local boys brought fresh oysters and lime to compliment our picnic fare.

It was a great place for the kids. They roamed around where they wanted and had a special place in the woods they called 'Blue Valley'. It was a secret place and only later did they take us there. It wasn't as beautiful as their memories but it was 'Their Secret Place'.

They had a dog, Skippy, and a Parrot, Jaunita, who sang 'Delores es mi Corazon' and talked a lot. She sang the scale leaving out a note. Our neighbor, Dave, made a hutch for their pet rabbits. Caballos presented them with a horse, Pinguino.

I don't know how we all crowded into that 3 bedroom, 2 bath house. We closed in the porch and made an extra room. Jim's parents left Venezuela soon after we moved in. They decided they had enough of Venezuela and Jim's Dad couldn't help in the business because Spanish proved to be a problem. We made plans to all go back together to Orlando where they planned to retire.

We got Baby Claire's American passport but the embassy was out of Venezuelan passports so we went on without it-a big mistake. When we got to the airport Jim handed the official the stack of passports. They said, "This baby was born in Venezuela. She is a Venezuelan and can't leave the country without a passport". Poor Jim had 8 passports, bunches of suitcases to look after and they all had to be brought back. We had to take the whole family to Caracas to get our little new Venezuelan her passport. We managed to get it in one day and get reservations the next day for Florida. Enter Mr Hyde. We always teased Jim that he turned into the famous counterpart of Dr Jekkyl when we traveled-No Wonder!

BARBADOS

The 1ˢᵗ time we went to Barbados was on our way back to Venezuela from the stateside vacation. After a vacation filled with going back and forth to Greensboro, Jim's parents, Pittsburgh and my parents we were ready for a carefree vacation to the islands. We had made arrangements to meet Rose and Bernie Texeira and stay for a week.

Barbados is a small island in the Caribbean and had been an English colony for years. The water was blue, the sands pure white and the people friendly.

By that time we had 4 girls the youngest, Claire, was 18 months. Rose and Bernie had 2. We rented 2 houses, hired a cook, a nursemaid and a driver. All spoke English with a charming accent-ending each sentence with "please". It took us a while to decide if they were asking a question or stating a fact. Karen upon reaching our little house on the sea walked to the beach and said, "I think I want to spend the rest of my life here". To this day she has always loved to be by the water.

The closest hotel was the Sandy Lane. Claudette Colbert, the old-time actress, had a home next door. It seemed like paradise to us.

Our vacation was one of the best we ever had. One day several little boys came by and asked if we would like them to sing for us. We invited them in and they proceeded to put on a show, songs and moon walking-a precursor to Michael Jackson. We all laughed till we cried and sent them on their way with a pocket full of money.

Many years later we decided to return and we took our daughter, Susan, and her husband back to see 'our island' again. They had gained independence from England and the people had changed-no more 'please' and they seemed unfriendly. We were so disappointed.

CHURCH

During these years we were very active in our church. We were privileged to have a minister, Al Deutsch, who became a dear friend and a man who influenced both Jim's and my lives. I will be eternally grateful to him for driving from Michigan to Woodland Park to give the funeral service for Jim. He is a man of my heart and a true gift from God to his parishioners. We had a service every Sunday. I always sang in the choir and both of us served on the church council. Al gave an early service in San Tome, drove to Anaco and several times a month went to Maturin to give a service there.

Jim couldn't carry a tune in a bucket although he wasn't always aware of this. One night I was getting ready to go to choir practice. Jim had another meeting and the girls wanted to know where he was going. He said, "I'm going to choir practice, I'm singing on Sunday". They all looked at each other, rolled their eyes and said, "Well, we aren't going Sunday".

ANDES HERE WE COME

One of the first trips we took with the children was over Easter vacation. I had always wanted to see more of Venezuela especially the Andes Mountains and Merida. There were always rumors of impending revolution in the air over holidays but we decided things seemed stable so we bundled up the 3 oldest girls leaving Claire with our very able and dependable Theodora and left for the vacation of a lifetime. All went well and the girls were having a great time. They had never seen mountain roads before and asked if they could just get out of the car and walk. We stopped several times-once in a beautiful mountain setting where they had a small zoo. We were all watching the monkeys and one of them dashed down to the fence and grabbed Barb's sun glasses off her face. We were all startled. The monkey ran up his perch and proceeded to twist the glasses into pieces while Barb cried her eyes out.

We finally made it to Mt Avila and took the teleferico up the Mountain. I think we were some of the first people on the ride since completion which wasn't a happy thought. We arrived at the top and it was freezing especially for 3 little tropical girls with only ruanas for coats that we bought in town. There was snow, a lot of rocks but the scenery was spectacular. Barb was walking around with her eyes shut and we asked her, "Why don't you open your eyes"? Her reply, "It's too cold to let my eyes out!" We got back on the lift and made it down safely-wondering how we ever had enough nerve to do it in the first place!

THE GOVERNMENT HAS FALLEN

Our trip home was uneventful until we reached Merida. The hotel staff ran out and announced, "The government has fallen". We were detained at the hotel for 3 days. The kitchen was open but no help to cook or serve. They had all been "liberated", so we helped ourselves to the food along with many other guests. No one was permitted to travel. Finally after 3 days, Jim said, "We're taking a chance that we can get through", so off we went! We were stopped and searched entering and leaving every small town-must have been 20 times. We had to get a special OK from the town mayors to buy gas.

The car finally developed a leak in the gas tank. Jim patched it up with soap (an old PA coal miner's trick) and on we went. About 1 mile from home we were stopped and the man at the road block wanted Jim's pen knife. Jim told him, "If you want some good knives, I just live 1 mile from here and I have lots of butcher knives and machetes-we all held our breath. He finally relented and let us go on our way and let Jim keep his pen knife.

We were so glad to get home we could have kissed the threshold on the way in. The moral of this story? If there are rumors of revolution it could happen!

Things settled down and we had a new dictator-much like the old one. Our only worry was how they would treat the oil companies. The revolution's purpose was to free the oppressed people. The next president oppressed them even more. Such is life in most of South America. It still holds true today.

JIM'S PROTÉGÉ, HANS JUCOM-WOLD

One day a young blond, blue eyed Norwegian boy who had been educated in Barbados walked into Jim's Gulf office looking for work. The only job available was 'Abrero 3rd Class' (digging trenches for pipelines). He said, "I'll take it". Jim was so impressed with him he found better work for him and when Hans asked Jim for help with his studies that he was doing on his own, Jim was glad to help. Hans even surpassed Jim's help. He worked for Jim until Jim went into business for himself then he quit Gulf, went to see Jim and told him, "I'm here to work for you".

Soon after that we heard of a program Gulf was sponsoring for Venezuelan employees. Jim talked Hans into going back to Gulf so he could be eligible. Hans was working for our old friend, Charlie Wheeler, and when the program came up, Charlie didn't want to let Hans go because he was such a good employee. Jim interceded and Charlie relented. Hans went off to the States and got a Masters degree from MIT. He then got a Doctorate and went back to work for Gulf in the States for many years. He worked for Dub Goins who told Maury Hans was the best engineer Dub ever had working for him. He ended up a professor of Petroleum Engineering in College Station (TX A&M). Needless to say we were very proud of him and all that he accomplished. When Hans heard of Jim's death he called and asked how I was doing.

SCHOOL DAYS

We were all startled when Mobil Oil announced they were closing their school to all 'outsiders'. Most of the service companies had families so this posed a huge problem. We started a small school for the young children at Gradys, a local Bodiquin (bar) and hired the wife of the local missionary, Mrs Ruth to teach. Finally we met to discuss the possibility of starting a permanent school which meant hiring teachers from the States and getting correspondence courses to guide the studies. Some of us had a little experience but it was a little over our heads organization-wise. By some great chance of luck we found a lady who was a retired school principal. She was in Venezuela with her husband who worked for NALCO. She took over and became the guiding light in the birth of Escuela Anaco, 1st-9th grades. We found a large unused warehouse building and all of the service companies went together and fixed it up into a proper school. We started hiring teachers through an ad in a Texas newspaper. So our school was born out of necessity and it turned out to be an excellent school at that. So good that Mobil decided to close their school and send their children to Escuela Anaco.

Looking back it's hard to believe that we accomplished so much, but the old saying, "necessity is the mother of invention" certainly proved true.

The cost was pretty high, $300 per child per month but most of the service companies paid the tuition. Small companies like ours suffered and with 3 in school it was a major expense.

Several women who had been teachers were there with their husbands had to get special permits to be able to work. Josephine Harper, a good friend of ours, had been a music teacher and directed our community choir was hired. She taught several subjects as did Renata Paragini. Renata taught Spanish and whatever else came up! They both had children the same age as ours and they became lifelong friends. Our Karen was one of 9 graduates from the 1st graduating class.

Basically, things ran smoothly-we made a few mistakes in hiring. One was a couple from California who became our first principal. His wife taught math. They were a little too liberal morally for the mostly conservative community. She was a beautiful blond. He was a nice guy but seemed to enjoy spanking little folks (especially girls) for infractions. My own daughter, Susan came home one day and said she took a spanking for a classmate who they all considered frail and too dainty to get spanked. Seemed a bit strange. We didn't know whether to applaud her caring or get upset. We let it go rather than cause trouble.

Another couple, Jerry and Margaret Coller were hired. He taught science and the kids loved him. He did experiments in class that really intrigued them and sparked their interest.

We could never figure out what happened (it was jealousy I think) but the principal said he was letting them go because he received a letter from Jerry's past school saying they had a very bad reputation there. He read it to the school board and they decided to terminate them. I was irate-I just couldn't believe the story. That summer one of our school board members went by and checked with the school. They said they hadn't written such a letter and that Jerry and Margaret were highly regarded. Of course by then it was too late to do much but let the principal and his wife go when they were confronted with the truth. We kept in touch with the Collers and the last we heard they were teaching in Belize and had written a tourist book on the area.

BALLERINAS

Life was pretty normal for us during these years. Along came Mme Gizelle from who-knows-where and said she wanted to open a ballet school. She had been a ballerina in Spain or so she said. Every child wanted to do ballet. She put on several shows after the first year that were really good. Susan did the 'Swan' and was wonderful-at least in our eyes. I usually helped with the costumes. Amazing what you can come up with when you are limited to a small store in the village for supplies most of which they never had heard of before. Some things we brought back from the States like ballet shoes and tutus. The customs officials wondering what possible use we would have for them in the 'interior'.

The 2 older girls took piano lessons. Karen did so well she played for church several times.

I was kept busy taking the kids back and forth to school, church choir, women's club and appearing in several musicals. One I especially remember was 'Black Face', a minstrel show which was hilarious. Not politically correct these days. We had theme parties such as Sadie Hawkens Day.

Jim and Susan McKee won the prize for their costumes as Fearless Fosdick and Pig Pen McSwine. We had hippie night, Gay Nineties night and lots of kids parties. Easter egg hunts and Christmas with Santa. One of the most entertaining was a Paris fashion show. Somehow we talked the men into modeling ladies clothing. Helping them dress as they gulped down drinks for courage was the experience of a lifetime. The show was a great success. We had 1 movie a week at the San Jaquin Club and a pool. My kids still today say I would only let them go to the movies if it was a Disney movie-not quite true but I was pretty strict on what they could watch. How times have changed. Movie night meant a soft drink for them which they never had at home.

All-in-all my kids had a pretty good place to grow up.

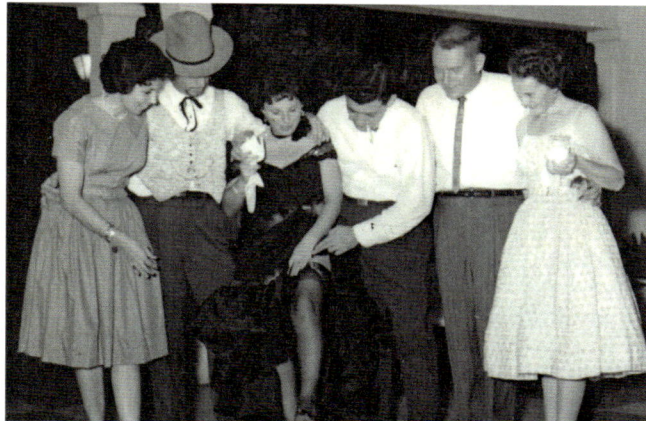

Can-can girl, Hippies, Fearless Fosdick, Moonbeam McSwine and the latest fashions

We were all healthy except for a few sore throats or ear aches. About this time I came down with a strange chest pain which, in retrospect, was probably a gall bladder attack. The doctors thought it could be TB (though all tests were negative) as they found a spot on my lung. I spent 6 weeks in bed to rest and took lots of pills when finally Dr Briceno took some more tests and found that it was histoplasmosis caused by breathing BAT DROPPINGS several months ago when we visited and explored a cave. He said if it doesn't kill you in 2 weeks, don't worry about it! I still have a scar on my lung which I have to explain every time I have chest x-ray.

After all this was over we decided I should go to New Orleans to Ochsner's clinic to make sure I was over the problems and the diagnosis was correct. So after many tests the verdict was, "You are in perfect health; the only thing we could find is that you are pregnant!" I called back to Jim and he thought I was kidding! SURPRISE

VACATIONS

Susan McKee and I decided to take a vacation to Barbados. We packed up the kids and rented a house, cook and baby sitter for a total of $50 a week. Joe and Jim were to meet us there. They were going to fly (we had our own planes by then) but the weather turned iffy, they got cold feet and flew commercial. I was all over my health scare and we had a great time. Barbados was still a beautiful island and the beaches are the best in the world.

Susan and Joe are still some of my favorite people. Joe was hurt in a car accident later and was permanently disabled with a brain injury. Susan is still looking after him 40 years now. She is surely a candidate for sainthood. (He died peacefully this year, 2013.)

We spent a lot of time planning vacations. So important being away from the family and the good old USA. One year we met Rose and Bernie Texeira in New York. They had never been to the states and we had great fun showing them NYC. It was the first time Rose had ever seen an elevator. We went to the favorite tourist places. We went to a famous night club where Bernie excused himself to go to the restroom. He returned with a funny look on his face. He had been met with an attendant offering a hot towel and a brush for his suit. He was obliged to tip him. His retort was, "Well, that's the first time I spent $2 to pee."

We traveled by car to Canada where they had family in Toronto. We stopped at a motel on the way. We were their first customers of the year and it was freezing. We ended up drinking the most part of a bottle of Guiana Rum that Bernie was taking to relatives!

All-in-all we had a great time. We met their families at a dinner club where we saw Ella Fitzgerald. She didn't impress us as much as she spent half of the time berating the musicians who played for her.

FLYING

About this time Jim decided to go in with our next door neighbor and buy a Cessna 172, the excuse being he could use it for business. In reality he had always wanted to fly since he joined the Air Force at 17 at the end of WW II. The flying club had come to town and all of our friends were taking lessons. Jim got his license and was happy as a clam.

I wasn't cutout to be Amelia Earhart. After a lot of persuasion and argument that I should know how to fly in case of emergency, I decided to give it a try. Our instructors were Venezuelans none of whom spoke English I remember the phrase 'naris arriba' (nose up) when landing so many times. On one occasion the instructor said, "Find a place to land". After much calculation I headed for what I thought was a road. It turned out to be a large pipeline. The instructor switched on the engine and said, "Now what?" My reply was, "Well, we now have engine power I think I'll go back to the airport". I finally soloed after 14 hours of instruction and I was pretty nervous. I remember thinking, "Grace, you have a family at home. What are you doing up here?"

I successfully did my 2 takeoffs and landings to the cheers of Venezuelan and American onlookers. They doused me with oil as was the custom and I had to ride home in the back of someone's pickup. Jim was out of town and when he returned he couldn't believe I had soloed. It was just as well-he would have been more nervous than I. That was the end of my flying career-I never took any more lessons.

Jim in the new Cessna Romeo Tango Kilo and
The trip to the Colombian border

TRINIDAD

One year we decided to go to Trinidad for Carnival. We loaded up our plane with all of the kids and were last in line to take off. Three other planes held our friends and all had pretty nice planes much faster than our Cessna. As we listened to the radio each plane reported landing as we flew on. Karen said, "Dad, we must be the slowest plane in the world."

We finally arrived and made our way to the Hilton Hotel. The Goens mixed up a Gott can full of rum punch and we proceeded to the stands to watch the parade of 'BANDS', groups of costumed locals. The costumes were unbelievable. We were told they started making them a year ahead. The whole island was awash with calypso music and we fell into the spell of the beat. Tuesday at midnight before Ash Wednesday it all stopped and Lent started. We could hardly walk in a normal stride after leaving. It took days to erase the calypso beat from our brains.

OFF WE GO FISHING

We used the plane to take many enjoyable trips and one I remember was taking our preacher's visiting father-in-law fishing. Jim and I and father and daughter took off for the wilds to show him some "real fishing" Upon arriving at the river he and Jim got into a dugout canoe and went to a back part of the river where the "big ones" were, leaving the two women to fish by themselves. We soon started catching fish and since we weren't sure how to take them off the hook, we devised a method of one of us stepping on the fish while the other would take it off the hook. When the men got back we had a huge stringer of fish and they hadn't had much luck with the 'big ones'.

Jim's flying buddy was Walter Idell, a German pilot during the war. He had a Grumman F4F fighter plane that he had converted for his own use. He was a professional pilot employed by Gulf Oil. He and Jim went fishing and exploring together and he taught Jim a lot about flying and landing in back country.

The virgin waters of Venezuela were loaded with pavon (peacock bass) and a fisherman's dream. Jim and friends went every chance they got and always came back with an ice chest full of fish. After getting the plane they were able to fly into remote places and I was finally able to join them in the fun.

We took the girls many times and Claire our youngest daughter even caught a 12 lb pavon with a little help from her dad. After the fish was landed she said, "That's it-I'm finished".

We had many memorable trips into the interior.

The big catch pavon (peacock bass) and Into the interior with indians

WATCH OUT-IT'S A SNAKE OR WORSE

One trip was organized by a Venezuelan employee of Jim's to the border of Colombia. On arriving with 4 other couples, they had planned a BBQ of beef and had it ready for us! We ate on banana leaves for plates. I don't remember if there was anything else to eat but the beef was pretty tough.

We were all a little edgy about being out in the bush. There was a small building there with a bed and a sofa. We strung our cinchurras (woven hammocks) for sleeping. It was very hot and we finally all got to sleep. It was pitch dark and during the night one of the Venezuelan men trying to make his way outside lost his balance and grabbed one of the ladies' legs. She let out a scream and the whole group sprang into action thinking some strange animal had attacked. The poor guy was in a corner completely humiliated and afraid we would hang him from the nearest tree!

The next morning everyone went in a different direction to catch fish. Ruth Goen and I decided to walk the edge of the river and try our luck. Ruth screamed, "Look out!" We were about to step on a huge anaconda sunning himself on the river bank. We hurried back to base camp and decided not to explore again by ourselves. It was quite an experience for all and we laughed like crazy telling the story when we got back to Anaco.

Many times the men encountered native Indians who had never seen a white man or an airplane before. They sometimes carried bows with poison arrows so the men were always careful watching out for any that looked 'hostile'. The Indians didn't speak Spanish so all communications were pretty much by sign language. They once brought a little girl to the 'strange men' for them to heal an eye infection. After much confusion the men gave her some antibiotic and tried to explain how to use it.

The plane was a great help in exploring the back country and finding new fishing grounds.

OFF TO EUROPE

One year we decided to see Europe. Our friends Sharon and Charlie Willmeth were going with us. We had various planning sessions and decided that Sharon and I would go ahead and do some shopping for the proper clothes for the trip. Chas and Jim would stay for that week in Venezuela and bring the kids to Miami. We would then take them to grandparents while we went to Europe. The men didn't anticipate traveling alone with children and they arrived in Miami completely exhausted.

Our trip to Europe was wonderful, London, Paris, Italy, Germany, Norway. We saw everything there was to see. We had a little trouble in Paris. Sharon tried to help with her high school French-but it was sadly lacking. We couldn't even figure out how to use the telephone at the train station. The French weren't much help. We saw so many shows-one, the Follies Bergerie, where Jim fell asleep with all of the topless beauties dancing in front of him.

Jim, Grace and Sharon Wilmuth

Jim, Grace, Sharon and Charlie

We returned to the States to pick up the children who made out famously with grandparents and back to Venezuela with many photos and many wonderful memories.

SILVER ISLAND

When we were in Venezuela we went, when possible, to Puerto La Cruz to the beach there. One beach was called 'Silver Island' the other 'Colorado'. The most memorable thing about Silver Island other than the crystal clear water and white sand were the little native boys bringing oysters and limes. We ate them by the dozens and managed to survive. One funny happening was during a water skiing venture. Our friend, Paul Koester, was skiing and thought he saw a shark following. He yelled, "Shark, Shark". The guy driving the boat thought he said, "Stop, Stop". So he cut the motor and Paul sank in the water with the shark which then he hoped was his imagination.

ANGEL FALLS

You may have heard about Angel Falls, the highest (3000 feet) falls in the world. We took a trip there with friends. We flew in and saw the falls from the plane-although I wasn't too comfortable flying so close in a mountainous area. Jimmy Angel crash landed at the top of the falls years ago and they were named after him. I didn't want my name added to the 'Lore of the falls'. There was a small camp there, Jungle Rudys; primitive rooms and chiweres (wart hogs) running around freely! The kids thought it was great.

Tame chiwere at Jungle Rudys at Angel Falls and
the new steamer with me in hard hat

VACATION FROM HELL

Our vacation next year was to be especially exciting leaving from Venezuela via the French Line through the islands and on to Puerto Rico to visit friends. We awoke in Anaco the day we were to leave to a thick fog. In all the years there we had never seen fog! No plane out that day! We drove 60 miles to Puerto La Cruz and flew to Caracas, from there a taxi to La Guira arriving late. We were told we had lost our reservations. There we were in the parking lot with luggage and 3 little girls; Jim tearing `his hair out and me sobbing.

Finally the cruise people said we could board but the first 2 nights would be first class and the next 2 steerage. We thought this over and decided it wouldn't be too bad. We could still eat in the 1st class dining room.

We made our way to the cabin, Barbara all the while asking when we were going to get on the boat every 10 minutes. It looked like a big hotel to her. The room was great, wood paneling, gold faucets. We had wonderful meals with huge fruits that we had never seen before and, of course, French cooking. We thought we had made a really good deal. WRONG!

Off we went on the third day "down below where you'd be the first to go" The room was bunk beds, a fan in one end of the cabin and a sink in the other. A port hole for a window with the water line very close. We all managed to get dressed in our best 'cruise clothes" and started to go up to dinner. We were locked in. No riff-raff allowed above! Jim called someone and we were allowed to enter the dining room then ushered back and locked in again. Luckily that was for only 2 nights and we survived.

We arrived in Puerto Rico after stopping in several islands, got off the ship and no taxi wanted to take us; too many kids and luggage. Jim, of course, lost his cool and shouted in Spanish that we never come to Puerto Rico again. I tried to calm him down and with the help of some local people standing by was able to find 2 taxis to take us to the hotel. The hotel manager said, "I'm very sorry, but we don't have any reservations for you; we're full". We had to load everything up and the manager found us another hotel.

The visit with friends was very enjoyable, we loved the island but we were getting anxious to get back to the good old USA. When we arrived in NY at the airport it was freezing and a light snow. The kids were all crying and we had to walk from the plane to the terminal outdoors.

We finally talked 2 taxi drivers into taking us to the hotel. The plane was late and we arrived at the Taft hotel at 11:00 PM. We stood in shock when they said, "You are too late we didn't save a room!" Poor Jim was finally speechless. He glared at the manager and said we would stay in the lobby. After a flurry of calls they told us they had found a suite of rooms at the Waldorf Astoria to which Jim said, "No, we can't possibly afford that" and they replied, "It's all taken care of; it will be the same rate". Off we went with 3 sleepy kids thinking we would probably be turned away. They must have realized they had an irate husband and a wife about to have a nervous breakdown. The Waldorf Astoria met us with good grace, clean beds and we realized we were at last safe.

The next AM Jim went to the Gulf office early and when I had the kids dressed we went down to eat breakfast. A nice old lady in the elevator was very taken with our little family and asked what we were doing in New York. I said, "My husband works for Gulf Oil and he is at the office" She said, "Oh yes, I think I own some of that company" She was a resident at the Waldorf.

The next two days we took the kids around to see New York. They weren't too impressed. They don't even remember it today!

After gathering our baggage, we headed for the train station to find that we were about to miss the last train to Pittsburgh. Jim gave the porter $20 and Dad's phone number and asked him to call with the arrival time in Pittsburgh. The porter did call and Dad was there to meet us. Our faith was somewhat restored in New Yorkers! I have no memory of the rest of that trip; it must have been uneventful!

SURPRISE

Enter John David Black born February 25, 1966 at the Mobil hospital in Anaco. Dr Bonillo was in attendance and was so excited to deliver a boy after our 4 girls that he gave out cigars. Somehow he thought it was all due to his expertise!

John arrived home under the watchful eye of 5 mother hens! They all still today think he can do no wrong.

Not too many couples our age had big families but we felt very lucky that we were able to raise 5 in a good environment and that they were all able to have a happy childhood. They have all turned out into wonderful adults and still are all the best of friends. We were asked several times if we were Catholic since we had such a large family-Jim's reply was, "No, we're just compatible-I'm comfortable and Grace is so pattable".

Karen, Susan, John and Claire

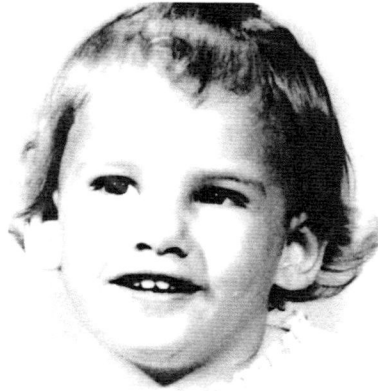

Barbara and rest of family before John

TROUBLE IN PARADISE

The financial situation was getting difficult about this time with the exit of another regime and take over by the people slowed the business down. The second workover rig was cancelled and the steamer was put on hold pending the new government's regulations. Jim and Joe McKee had a small car distributorship that was not doing well and Joe had a terrible accident on the way to inspect the steamer. We were pretty much using all of our income for school, rent and necessities so Jim decided to make a trip to the States to see what other opportunities were available for him. He came back and announced that he was offered a great deal to rehire with Gulf and it would include the previous 7 years toward retirement. We would be leaving for Bolivia. When I told my doctor we were going to Bolivia, he said, "I'm so sorry for you."

ADIOS VENEZUELA

This was our last Christmas greeting as we were leaving Venezuela.

'Twas the night before Christmas
      and all through the casa
Not a creature was stirring;
      caramba! Que pasa!
The stockings weren't hung
      and the house all bare
'Cause the Blacks were en route
      to heavens knows where!
Mama with her suitcase,
      papa with good cheer??
Were wondering where
      they would settle next year.
Should they take a few cosas
      and send all they dare?
Or pack everything,
      even long underwear?
John's saving a stocking
      to hang where we are
In hopes that St. Nick
      brings a new racing car.
In a giant big sleigh
      drawn by eight jet reindeer
The chicas are coming
      to spend the New Year.
But wherever Santa finds us
      we wish you one thing:
All the happiness and joy
      only Christmas can bring!

The Blacks

BOLIVIA

Santa Cruz serenaders and delivery cart

We were pleasantly surprised; many of the people there we knew, a nice climate, although it was very primitive. There was a golf course and a lot of friendly people just wanting to help us get settled. The roads were unpaved, not much in the way of a grocery store and no bread to buy.

We stayed in a hotel and waited for our shipment to arrive.

By this time Karen was staying with Jim's sister till we could find a proper boarding school and Susan was getting ready to go to the 9th grade too. My nest was getting empty!

ALMOST EMPTY NEST

We found the boarding school in Orlando; Howey Academy close to Jim's parents.

I wasn't quite ready to give them up at such a young age and had many reservations about it, but off they went ready for a new adventure without any qualms at all. I was feeling a little let down that my girls were so anxious to leave home. They were able to come home for holidays and summer vacations, so it wasn't the end of the world although I was pretty blue for a month or so until I heard they were doing well and loved it in Orlando.

BLACK AND WHITE

One day at the club we met Sandy White. He was the AID rep for Bolivia. He was being transferred and had a very nice house on the edge of town-a swimming pool, tennis court, guest house and fruit trees. He said we could move in although he didn't know when they would replace him. We decided it would be better than living in the hotel so we took him up on the offer. Our things arrived from the States and we lived there the entire time we were in Bolivia; 2 years. We kept the power plant running for our rent (it furnished power for 2 other houses) and were very happy there, we considered our selves very lucky.

We only had Claire and John at home. Claire found friends she loved and John was still a toddler.

There was an election going on in the States. I think it was Humphrey and Nixon. So we decided to have an election of our own. We chose candidates for each party-had hats, streamers and ballots. Our candidate didn't make it to the election-he was passed out under the table. I guess the stress of running for president was too much for him!

Jim enjoyed his job. Claire was enjoying school so John was the only one left with me. We found a cook who made delicious bread and life was going well.

Jim inherited a great bird dog from Lou Ramsey who was leaving Bolivia and we had another small dog for the kids. We had a nice church community and attended weekly.

A BAD DAY AT BLACK ROCK

It was Sunday, a beautiful summer day. We came home from church and Claire and her friends wanted to go swimming. The pool had a fence and padlock. They all got into their suits and opened the gate. John had his little football life saver on. I said we would change into our suits and be out in a minute. That minute was one of the longest of my life. Claire was screaming, "John has drowned". We rushed to find him face down in the shallow part of the pool with his "football" on top of the water. Jim immediately started CPR and I ran inside, called a friend and asked (NO, TOLD) her to find the doctor and bring him quickly.

John's face was blue and he wasn't breathing. Jim inadvertently turned him over putting pressure on his stomach and John gagged, threw up water and started breathing. They found the doctor on the golf course-he rushed to the house and by the time he got there John was smiling and asking to go back swimming. The only lasting problem was John's refusal to get his hair washed or get water on his head!

It seemed that Bolivia was going to be a pretty good place after all this traumatic experience. We had a great house, school was going good for Claire and Jim had a good bird dog!

GOOD OLD USA

Karen, Susan and Barb were coming for the summer and invited 2 boyfriends to Bolivia for 2 weeks. The boys arrived in the middle of the summer and the girls had great fun showing them around. As luck would have it, the power plant went out.-we had no electricity and we had to carry water in from the pool to flush toilets. This turned out to be a really FOREIGN experience for 2 city boys. After they returned we got a thank-you note, "Dear Mr & Mrs B. Thanks for the great vacation-it really made us appreciate the good old USA!"

SERENADES & FATTED CALF

As always there were other teenagers visiting their parents for the summer and a steady stream of Bolivian boys interested in the "Americanas". One night after we had all turned in I heard music from outside. It was a group of Bolivian boys serenading the girls by their window. Needless to say, the girls were quite impressed!

One family, Chief New, decided to kill a "fatted calf" and have a big BBQ when their son arrived. Great preparations were made-the calf put on a giant spit and turned on a fire. It rained and took a much longer time than expected-the meat was done on the outside but not edible on the inside.

Chief was quite a character. He was an Oklahoma Indian and had a very rare sense of humor. We were all at the party when one of the women who was quite impressed with her "I'm so smart attitude" asked Chief what tribe he was from. "Well", he said, "I'm from the Fakawee tribe"-her reply was, "Well, I've studied a lot about American Indians and I never heard of that tribe". "Oh yes", he said. "They are a very old and respected tribe, here's how they got their name. The chief of the tribe was out with a hunting party in a new area so he went to the top of the hill and said, "Where the f—are we?"". The poor woman was flabbergasted and never asked Chief a serious question again

BAD NEWS

Jim came home with bad news. Mark McKee who was looking over our interests in Venezuela had been shot and killed by a distraught Venezuelan whose daughter had run away from home. It happened in a parking lot of a local restaurant. There was some sort of car accident between the 2 cars and Mark who was fluent in Spanish got out of his car and yelled at the man who pulled out a gun and killed Mark on the spot.

It was a great shock to us. Mark was a great young man with a great sense of humor. He had been discharged from the army on his parent's request to take over their company in Joe's place who was suffering from a brain injury due to an accident on the way to the steam unit.

Jim went back to Venezuela immediately to make arrangements for the workover rig and steamer. He turned the steamer over to Susan McKee and the rig to a partner who had a small interest in the business. Susan did a great job in getting work for the steamer but Sr Polombo kept all of the income from the rig and it finally burned down.

A friend later went out to the location and salvaged a large bolt from the fire site. We now use it for the most expensive paper weight in history.

Venezuela became a distant memory of shattered dreams.

BACK TO BOLIVIA

Bolivia, meanwhile, was doing well. Jim liked his work; he was out in the field a lot. The next crisis in the life of the Black family was about to happen.

WE'RE OUT OF HERE! BUT NOT BY CHOICE!

Jim was in the field and the great government takeover was about to happen: nationalization of Gulf Oil Company by the Bolivian government.

The army marched into the offices and confiscated everything, cars, paperwork, radios, etc. All personnel were relieved. Jim in the field was the last man left with transportation. He was unaware of the situation until he radioed in and got orders to shut down the gas plant. After doing this he was held for awhile. His pickup was taken and he was escorted home.

In the middle of that night the army came to our house looking for the President who had escaped. They thought we might be hiding him in the guest house. They believed Jim's story that he hadn't seen anyone. He was very convincing and we were all in the house wondering what would come next.

TIME TO GO

We were given one week to leave. The company secured 2 planes and we were told we could take only 2 suitcases. Everything else would stay in "hopes" that we would get our things at a later date. To our amazement we did; the exception being pastel portraits that we had done of all of our children (something to remember us by I guess).

We sold everything we could; furniture, appliances, a Volkswagen Bug and tried to decide what we could cram into 2 suitcases. I laid out everything I thought I couldn't part with on the bed. It would have filled 10 suitcases! We finally narrowed it down- I kept 2 crystal dishes of my Mom's and that was it! We were scheduled for the 2nd plane out.

SO LONG, FAIRWELL, AUF WIEDERSEHEN

That last night we and a group of our friends got all of our precious shrimp that we had been saving in our freezers, all of our good whiskey and had a party! I had a bottle of Bailey's Irish Cream that I was saving for a special occasion and this seemed to be that occasion. The last I remember of that night I was singing "Tip Toe Though the Tulips" in a very strange voice that wasn't my own.

We had to find homes for our pets and that great bird dog Jim had inherited from Lou Ramsey. Jim was so attached to that dog I was a little worried that he would take the dog and leave me.

Gulf agreed that we could turn in all of our Bolivian money that we got for selling our things and would be reimbursed later. I met Jim in town after he left the office with enough money to buy 3 pieces of jewelry. I still have it as a reminder of my good judgment in buying "gold". Two of those pieces went to my granddaughter, Jessie, when she graduated from college.

On the road again

OFF WE GO

We boarded the plane ready to face what came next deciding to stop off in Venezuela to see friends. Most of the other people went off to Miami where they were put up in a hotel. Gulf even hired psychiatrists to council all who needed help facing the loss of home, pets and belongings.

Our trip via Santa Paula was uneventful. Claire and John were anticipating a new adventure and taking everything in their stride. We were about to have one of the most traumatic 2 months of our lives.

A HAPPY HOMECOMING TO VENEZUELA-OR SO WE THOUGHT

Upon arriving in Caracas we met Bill Shivers one of our best friends from our Anaco days. He was returning from a church conference and his wife, Lucille, was staying on a few more days. We were overjoyed to meet him at the airport and made plans to travel back to Anaco together. We boarded the plane which had one stopover in San Tome not knowing what a horrible event was about to take place. Bill and Jim got off to make arrangements for transportation from Anaco airport and Bill invited us to stay with them when we reached Anaco. Our plan was to stay a week.

When they came back on the plane Bill was visibly shaken and Jim was helping him to his seat. The telephone call to Anaco was not good. There had been a terrible accident-16 children going on a birthday picnic were riding in a crew car when a flat bed truck missed a curve and turned over on top of them. Several of the children were killed immediately and some were in the hospital. Bill's one boy was dead and they weren't sure about the other one. Melissa Everett, Claire's best friend and next door neighbor for many years was in the hospital with fatal injuries.

All of these children were classmates of Claire's and had we taken the first plane out of Bolivia she would have been along with them for the party. The Good Lord was looking after us!

The next few days were an unspeakable heartbreak for the whole small community. We rushed to the hospital to see Melissa and she lived only one day. Bill's other son wasn't on the trip so he was safe. As it turned out every other child sitting on each side of the row was killed; 6 killed 3 with brain injuries and the rest spared. What a horrible tragedy. The driver's own child was killed and he had to bear the guilt for many years even though he wasn't at fault. Only God knows the reason, if there was one.

We stayed on for several more weeks and baby sat the Shivers' 18-month old daughter, Carla, while they went to the States to bury their son.

I don't know what effect all this had on Claire. We never talked too much about it but it must have been a significant occurrence in her young life.

Years later at our 50th anniversary Bill got up and said, "The Lord sent 2 special angels to console us at that time." I can't relate to being an angel, but it really was an unusual happening that we arrived on the scene that day. So maybe God did send us.

We left Venezuela saddened but with the realization that in life's many experiences, friendship is the most important.

BOGOTA – WATCH YOUR WATCH

When we got to the States we found that we were assigned to Bogota Colombia. We were to stay in the hotel until our furniture and personal effects arrived. After several days of headaches we began looking for a house and found a very nice one. The things from Bolivia did arrive however and it took forever.

Our friends from Bolivia, the Vondrens, were there too so we were able to wait together for our things to arrive. We stayed at the Tecundama Hotel which commiserate was one of Bogota's nicest and waited patiently for things to arrive. We all got hooked on a local TV show, "Simplemente Maria", and hurried back from wherever we were to watch the next episode and have our favorite desert, Peach Melba. Yoya, a Bolivian, and Bob, an American geologist, had one child and when Susan, Karen and Barbara came for the summer, we had some great times together.

We finally got our shipment and moved into our house. Our friends, Ernie and Molly Haynes and Chief New were there. Somewhere we became the owners of a little French Poodle named "Ami". We were settled in for a nice stay. WRONG-we were there a little over a year and the Great Father Gulf said, "We need you in Argentina".

Columbia was a great place although known for professional thievery. It wasn't too unusual for the theft of your car and then a phone call back ransoming it for a not too unreasonable price. One story we were told was that a thief would come up to your car at a stop light and grab the watch off your hand (no air conditioning then). One clever man decided just to wear his watch on the other arm. The thief came up, burned his hand with a cigarette and when he instinctively grabbed his painful hand, the watch was then stolen from his other arm.

We were told not to put anything near windows and never open the door to a stranger. One day the maid started yelling, "Get out of here." She told me someone was stealing the Shasta daisies I had planted along the edge of the yard. I was rather embarrassed but ran outside just as the woman boarded the bus. She had dug out several plants while waiting for the bus and carried them off with her.

We went to several bullfights which I found very exciting. We heard they were going to have "Children's Day" with clowns and young bulls, so we gathered up all of our kids and went to see the show. It was a very exciting show-young matadors, clowns, paper built house in the ring which they coaxed the bulls through, all great fun-then they killed the bulls! We thought this would be a horrible experience for the kids but it didn't seem to bother them at all!

ON THE ROAD AGAIN ARGENTINA

Finally it was time to be "On the road again". We said goodbye, packed up again and found a home for our new puppy, Ami. She found a wonderful home with the Vondrens. We visited them years later in Texas and Ami was still alive at 17. She became a real Ami (friend in French) to their family and got to travel to many places with them.

Argentina was going to be a little different than most places for us: there would be only 3 American families; 1 geologist, 1 drilling manager and Jim as manager. We arrived in Buenos Aires full of grand expectations as we had heard it was much like a European city. We stayed a short time in BA and met some interesting people. One was our landlord who had a ranch outside the city. He invited us to see his place and we gladly accepted. He was German-tall, handsome, with striking blue eyes and had been in Argentina many years. I always suspected he might have been one of the German military who escaped to Argentina after the war. At any rate, he was very kind and made our short stay very enjoyable.

ARGENTINA "GENERAL ALVEAR"

We traveled on to General Alvear, a small town in western Argentina. There we found many Italians who had been there at least 3 generations. There was a winery established in San Rafael very close by and we were about 50 miles south of Mendosa.

We stayed at the Grosso Hotel-1 room for Jim and me, 1 for the kids and 1 for the luggage. We were a curiosity being the first Americans most of the people had ever seen! The owner's son had a saying which we have never forgotten: "Despues del Ano Nuevo" (after the new year). This was used for anything that needed to be done later. It comes in handy.

The Drilling Manager, Jr Cox, Helen and their 2 children, a boy and a girl about the age of our kids, arrived. Larry Littlefield and his new bride, Isabel, arrived.

We all found housing. Ours turned out to be very nice. It was owned by an older couple and they were adding an apartment for family. We convinced them to finish it and rent the entire place to us. The American dollars looked good to them at the time but later, their money got devalued and we ended up with a pretty good deal.

The house had a pool but no water so it was not usable. There was a fireplace in the kitchen and living room and a copper water heater which was heated by a wood fire. We melted it down in no time.

The owner had a couple working for them and they lived out back in a small house so we hired them on; she for the house, he for the garden, feed the few chickens and keep the fireplaces going. One day we looked outside and found the chickens hanging in burlap bags on the clothes line. "What is this?" we asked. The gardener replied, "They stopped laying and this will start them again." That winter they had their first snow in years and we nearly froze. We bought some small butane heaters and walked around with them wherever we went. The bedrooms were so cold it took a lot of determination to get in bed under the cold sheets.

Finally our things arrived and we were able to hook up a regular stove, washing machine and hot water heater.

SCHOOL DAYS GOOD OLD GOLDEN RULE DAYS

Our next chore was what to do about school. We decided to do home schooling from Correspondence School Department of the University of Nebraska. That lasted 2 months. Susan had decided to come to Argentina to finish her last year. I have a new appreciation for anyone who does home schooling.

We put a notice in the BA newspaper for a teacher and, lo and behold, we got an answer; Anita Lane. She was in Argentina visiting a schoolmate from Ames, Iowa, who had moved to Argentina and she wanted to stay on. She arrived shortly and we rented a small house for her and a school room. Gulf paid her salary and housing and she worked out really well. The kids got their lessons and did their homework!

NEW HOURS FOR DINNER

Dinner hours are drastically different in Argentina. Most Argentines have a tea time small meal around 3:00 and don't eat or start a party till 10:00 or 10:30 PM.

Susan struck up a friendship with the young Argentine crowd. She was to be home by 12:00. We had to go hunting for her at 1:00 AM. She complained that no one did anything till 11:00 after dinner so we had to modify our "come home time" till 1:00 AM.

The local veterinarian who was mainly caring for the cattle had a son, Billy, who became a regular visitor and he volunteered to doctor our adopted cat (rescued out of a tree at 1:00 AM). The cat seemed sick and we decided it had worms. Billy's medication caused the cat to race around the pool meowing. It disappeared never to return. I guess its medicine was for a much larger animal.

While we were all living at the hotel, John became enamored with all things cowboy. He had his cowboy boots that Dusty Peebles brought to him while we were still in Bolivia. They were much too large but he still insisted on wearing them. They ended up with turned-up toes like harem slippers. He had a cowboy hat and one of the Argentines men gave him a cap pistol called, "Mato Gato" (kills cats). That, of course, was his prized possession. He roamed around the halls all suited up in his cowboy gear and was the darling of the hotel.

The men were busy with their jobs; mainly to drill 27 wells in an agreement with the Argentine government. They were pretty sure there was no hope in finding oil-sure enough after our assignment was over-27 dry holes.

The oil workers came and went through the rancher's property and many times forgot to close the gates which is a no-no in cattle country. One day at breakfast we were told that one of the ranchers was irate and coming to town with a gun. It was Jim's duty to keep everyone happy in town so, nothing to do but wait till the rancher arrived. While having our café con leche and medea lunas, John arrived and decided to shoot off his cap gun. Thinking the rancher had arrived guns blazing, Jim jumped up, scooped up John and told him never to shoot that d—thing again.

All turned out peacefully-the rancher was placated with the promise of a cattle guard and a water well! Poor John was slightly bewildered at all the commotion he had caused.

The ladies had to find something to do-what better than go to the market where vegetables were very scarce-except for potatoes, carrots and tomatoes. They did have wonderful peaches in season. We heard of a Japanese colony that raised strawberries so we went out and bought more strawberries than we could possibly eat and made arrangements with a local store to freeze them-there were still some left when we departed!

The beef was wonderful. BEFE was the main staple of their diet. We decided to buy a half of beef and have it butchered at the local market. I went with my beef chart to direct the operation. The Argentines don't cut the meat leaving any bone in-it is all cut away from the bone and difficult to see what cut it is. Each piece that the butcher cut he explained to the curious bystanders, "See, this is the way Americans cut meat." He had never heard of a T bone steak!

Fish was unheard of except at Easter and chicken was pretty much avoided. Goat meat was common and was very good especially BBQed. We visited Mendosa when we first arrived and were treated to a huge goat BBQ by Macobar Service Company.

Jim decided to go out to a local ranch and pick out a goat for a BBQ. He took John along and they picked a small one out and brought it home. John was OK with the idea although I thought he shouldn't have been part of that procedure; he might have been ruined for life. He survived and has become, along with the Bertsch boys, avid hunters.

We took a trip to Bariloche. The women flew and the men went down the river in a boat and had a great fishing trip. It was a big deal for us-a real movie (where Isabel nearly got trampled to death) and some very nice restaurants.

Our first Christmas we decided to take a trip to the mountains. All 3 families took off with turkeys and a small Christmas tree. Jim managed to get 2 work trailers and we chose a beautiful spot to set up. We all went down to the lake and were the first ones there after the road was cleared. We caught lots of trout which Isabel prepared for us when we got back to camp.

Jim managed to get a fly hook caught in his ear and Karen was the only one with enough nerve to pull it out.

Back at camp we had a delicious trout dinner. On Christmas day we BBQed the turkeys on a spit.

That day a gaucho rode up and we gave him a bottle of wine which we kept cold in the little stream nearby. He seemed so happy to get the wine and rode away with a smile on his face!

The gaucho rode away with a bottle of wine and
dinner in Buenos Aires at Churascos

Years later the Littlefields went back to see Alvear and rode up to our camp site. The exact spot had been made into an exclusive ski resort.

Helen Cox had been a tennis champ at school so she volunteered to teach us to play. None of us made the grade and she finally gave up! We rode bikes everywhere and had morning exercise every other day.

The kids had regular school hours and were doing well. My Spanish improved immensely while there as I was forced to use it daily.

John started in the local school KINDER run by nuns and he was fluent in Spanish. That worked well until their Independence Day celebration. The KINDER class was to perform a song on stage. John refused to go on. After much persuasion we finally got him on stage and he stood there crying the whole performance. After the holiday he refused to go back to school. We took him kicking and screaming and dropped him off at school. Soon they called and said we would have to come and get him. We still don't know exactly why he balked but we decided to keep him home as we found out that we were going back to BA; Jim was to take the manager's job until Gulf closed down operations.

There was some unrest in Argentina at this time and before we left Avear someone painted a sign next to the office, "DEATH TO THE AMERICANS" Jim was not too worried as he had good relations with everyone there (almost everyone). We later discovered there had been a kidnapping of another oil company exec and Gulf had received threats so they decided to move the manager out, close his house and we were to rent another house.

John still has his little notebook in which he was learning to write, "Este es me mama" "Este es mi papa" and drawings to illustrate the words

TANGO FANDANGO

We said our goodbyes to the community which had accepted us with open hands and hearts. Anita Lane went back to live with her friends on a ranch in western Argentina. We kept contact with her for a long time. Her friend came to Alvear before we left and we went out to a club dancing. He was an expert at the Tango. Anita was able to keep up with him. I, on the other hand tried, but I can't say I passed the test!

BACK TO BA

We arrived back in BA and were able to find a nice house and inherit the household help who had worked for the previous manager. We were set up and hoping to stay in civilization for awhile.

Claire and John were enrolled in the American School. John finally decided that school wasn't so bad although they had to put him in special English class. He hung on to Claire like a baby kangaroo for the first 3 weeks. Poor Claire couldn't make a move without him. After the first few weeks he was anxious to go on the bus every day.

Upon arriving in BA we found the McKessons already there and we became reacquainted with them and their son, Warren. Warren asked Claire to her first prom. It was a big event in her young life. Nancy and Chuck played a big part in my life many years later.

Life in BA was great. Jim came and went to the office via train and once in a while I met him after work after a day of shopping. That's when I learned about the Argentine custom of pericos. While walking down the street men along the way would say things like, "I never knew a flower could walk". All very complimentary although you couldn't acknowledge them or they would follow you all over town. It did a lot for your ego!

There was more political unrest and we were there when Juan Peron and his wife returned to BA. She, Isabel, tried to become a new Evita but never made the grade. Evita was thought of as a saint. She died very young but when Juan was President she gave her all to the Argentine poor.

Unfortunately, our stay was rather short and soon we were to be transferred to Nigeria. The job in BA was complete and a few were left to finish negotiations on the pipeline. What would Nigeria hold? I could hardly <u>not wait</u>.

DON'T CRY FOR ME ARGENTINA

When we left Argentina we stopped in Rio de Janeiro. Our friends, the Littlefields were with us. It was a breathtaking sight and we enjoyed the trip. Isabel spoke Portuguese so she did most of the talking. Jim spoke Spanish to everyone since it was his only foreign language and, surprisingly, it was usually understood. But we couldn't understand their replies!

The Littlefields have been some of our closest friends through the years and to this day they have opened their home to Maury and me when we come to Houston. Their little boy, Davy, is now a grown man and a deep sea diver. Their Paul is working for Chevron.

We stopped off in London on the way to Nigeria as our shipment came through there and we had to sort out what we wanted to take and leave the rest in storage in London. I thought at the time it sure would be nice to live there one day but Jim's job had always been getting oil out of the ground and London didn't fit that scenario.

NIGERIA WEST AFRICA

We arrived in Nigeria in high hopes that it wouldn't be as bad as we had heard. Sure enough, it was. One story that sums it all up-a lady coming to join her husband asked the taxi driver, "What is that terrible smell?" to which he replied, "That's s—, Madam"!

Maybe it wouldn't be too bad; there was a house waiting and our things arrived quickly. Our assignment was to go to Port Harcourt. Gulf was building a new camp there. We didn't unpack our things right away-the job didn't materialize and when we finally unpacked there was Jim's shotgun right on top which was to have been left in London. It came through customs without any trouble and a local Doctor got him a permit right away. They were very strict on firearms: while we were there they confiscated a BB gun and BBs and threw the man in jail!

We got Claire and John started in school and went about getting settled in and meeting a lot of new people some of whom became lasting friends. The Hammonds, Maury and Sally; Jim and Linda Coapland, Pat and Jim Craton, and guess who? Our old friends, Ernie and Mollie Haynes.

Many of them owned a boat of some kind, so, nothing to do but buy a boat. Our first boat was a disaster. We bought it used and had nothing but trouble. It splashed a rooster tail all over the person riding in the back seat; guess who that was? Jim had convinced me I needed to ride back there to balance the weight!

We finally bit the bullet, bought a new boat and zoomed up the river without problems.

20 BEACH CLUB

There was the 20 Beach Club and the Motor Boat Club where we spent week ends. The 20 Beach Club was upriver and had 20 members. The members all had thatched roof huts. There was a waiting list and when the Haynes left, the Hammonds and Blacks bought their hut. It turned out to be a life saver for the men just to get out of Lagos for awhile. Upon arriving at the club we unloaded the ice chests and food for the day and it was carried up to the huts by the native women on their heads. The native men helped load up but basically did nothing else. That was women's work!

Women's work

We had many happy days there and it helped make life bearable. The men played volleyball and the games became rather serious at times depending on how much beer was consumed. The Black-Hammond hut was the center of many BBQs and card games. Little did I know that our lives would come together in an unusual way many years later.

There was another nice beach close in and a place called Bar Beach. During our stay Bar Beach held many public executions. They were televised and huge crowds turned out to watch the big show yelling their approval after each poor soul was shot. Not quite civilized, methinks.

We had a little poodle, Beau, and he and John became great friends. Beau played a game with John every day. I would give Beau a doggie bone and he would hide it till John came home from school and then put it in the middle of the doorway and growl showing his teeth if John tried to walk though the doorway. Beau ran outside and was killed by a passing car. We were heartbroken to lose him.

While in Nigeria Karen and Barbara were to come for the summer and wanted to see some of Europe on the way so we sent them money and Euro rail passes expecting them to arrive in a couple of weeks. We waited and worried when they didn't arrive figuring that they surely had been sold into the white slave market or something just as bad. They finally arrived after a month. They had been just about everywhere-ate bread and cheese-stayed in hostels-slept some nights going back and forth on the train and arrived at the London airport without a penny left-they hadn't counted on the exit fee. A good Samaritan paid for them and they arrived OK.

Festac was to be held in Nigeria that year and many pains were taken to prepare the town and grandstands-it turned out to be pretty much a fiasco. Traffic was backed up for miles and the events were not quite what were expected. The best solution for us was to stay home.

The American Embassy had a huge party for visiting guests and some of the oil company execs were invited. The ambassador, a black man, gave the welcoming speech and one of our visitors, a woman, proceeded to berate the embassy and gave a long discourse on the American Negros having been raped by the slave master and held in capture for many years. It was a very uncomfortable moment at what was supposed to be a welcoming party for visitors. When we heard the story many of us would have gladly paid her way to come and live in Nigeria for a year!

THE ART SCENE

I entered into the art scene making jewelry mostly from trade beads and ivory. The manager of Gulf decided to have an art show displaying paintings, etc., that Gulf personnel were doing in their spare time so I decided I would try pastels again and entered about 15 pictures. Much to my amazement I sold quite a few of them. Some of my old art training came in useful and I was slightly surprised that anyone would actually buy one. I went back to making jewelry and made a nice little profit on my creations. I still make jewelry today and have a collection of beads that takes up a large corner of my game room. I just can't pass up a pretty string of beads-It's an addiction!

I got involved in a weekly art show with my next door neighbor, Vivian Cox. She was showing art from local artists on Friday afternoons from 3-6 PM. It started out on a small scale and in no time became very popular with the foreign community. About this time I started making jewelry from trade beads; colorful ceramic beads that had supposedly been used years ago trading for goods much like the trinkets traded to the American Indians.

My jewelry became so popular that I recruited a friend to help me and we designed many necklaces all different from the beads. We then started using ivory pieces cut and shaped by local artisans. I had some time to do some pastels after a long absence from drawing.

Most of the beads we bought at the local market or from vendors at the hotels. Sometimes vendors came to the house selling beads, artifacts and ivory tusks. The chevron bead was very popular. It is a red, white and blue bead and very pretty. You can still find them in the U.S. and they are usually very expensive.

The local market where we bought many beads was pretty bad. You practically had to stop breathing to withstand the stench. There was an open sewer running along the market place. You weren't allowed to take pictures as there was a juju belief that it might rob the person in the picture of his soul. A few pictures were permitted and they showed unique native Nigerians in their turbans and native dress with a lovely little stream running by!

Karen came to stay with us after graduating from the University of Florida mid- term. Claire and John were still home and Susan and Barb came for the summer.

Somehow the Marine contingent at the Embassy discovered we had 3 daughters and before the girls came they started being very friendly with John (John was in the first grade). They took him to movies and came over to play with him. John never knew he was the open door to our house so they could be there when the girls arrived! The house was bombarded by marines while the girls were there and one never knew who would be at the door to see whom!

One caller was a young Swede, Bengt Eld, who was with a Nigerian cement company. He had a great sense of humor and we all really liked him. He was always broke and borrowing money from the Marines. However any day now his ship loaded with cement was due into port. A major highway and bridge construction project was underway and the port was overwhelmed with as many as 400 ships loaded with cement waiting for berths. Bengt's was one of them.

Karen got a job at the American Embassy and was planning on going back with us on summer vacation but Bengt had stolen her heart. When we left for the States she went with us but was determined she would come back. The embassy offered her a full time job when she returned and so she did-much against my better judgment. Lesson #1: You might as well hold your breath where love is concerned!

The next thing on our agenda was a wedding.

THE WEDDING

How do you plan a wedding in a place like Nigeria? Somehow we did with the help of many friends. No florist, no caterers, no gowns to buy. I can't really remember how Karen got her dress. I think we went back to the States with her and we bought her dress and 3 brides-maid dresses for her sisters. Anyway, we got though it all; picking flowers from trees, using dried heather for the bridesmaids which we carried back from the States. A local Japanese lady made a beautiful silk orchid for Karen's bouquet.

The wedding was held at the Nigerian Episcopal Church in Lagos and the reception in the back yard of our next door neighbor. We found a native man to play the piano. The bride was beautiful. Jim, Bengt and Bengt's friend found dinner jackets somewhere and they all looked very handsome. I cried at this wedding for some reason-maybe a premonition that only a mother can have.

John wore a white suit and was the ring bearer-he was quite taken with all of the notoriety. He was in so many of the wedding pictures that Bengt said, "It looks like we already had a child." Jill Coapland was the flower girl. The day and evening were perfect. It was the first wedding that had ever taken place in the expatriate community in Nigeria.

OFF TO DAHOMEY

We were always looking for some diversion to take us out of Lagos. Jim commandeered a company plane to take the Hammonds, Texieras and us to the neighboring country of Dahomey for a long weekend. On takeoff for returning to Lagos, the luggage door opened and Jim motioned to the pilot who brought the plane to a screeching halt into a ditch off the side of the runway. No damage except a few shattered nerves.

As soon as we got settled in the hotel to wait for a replacement plane, we walked the town and spotted a restaurant where they were unloading a shipment of fresh fruits. The celery caught our eyes since it was unheard of in Lagos. We tried to buy some but the manager said we could only have 2 bunches. We took them back to the hotel, washed them and ate them then and there- six people munching away like happy rabbits.

Strange experiences in Lagos were plentiful. We all had household help; most had been trained by the British. They all had white uniforms and we were madam and master. The men liked the master part!

MAURICE

Our houseboy was Maurice. He was a good, faithful servant during all of our stay there. He was a good cook too which was a plus and we considered ourselves lucky to have him.

The servants were provided with a room at the back of the house and food-they usually cooked their own.

During one period, Maurice became very lazy and listless. I finally had to talk to him to see what was happening. His explanation was, "I got married, Madam". Seems like he had a new young bride in his quarters and his strength was being depleted-not enough left to do his household chores!

My jewelry business and the Art Show were taking a lot of my time. My neighbor left Lagos and I was doing the show myself. We did play a lot of bridge and I was really enjoying it. Both ladies and couples bridge-there were a lot of good players many with master points, so we learned a lot about the game.

HOMELESS AGAIN

About that time the owner of our house decided he wanted our house and the one next to us back from the company. We needed to find ourselves some sort of company housing. The only place available at the time was an apartment on the 2nd floor on the other island.

Jim was out of town –he was doing a week on, week off at Port Harcourt. Our old friends, the Texieras were coming to live in Nigeria so I had a "tea" for Rose and all of the Gulf ladies were there. I had to call the landlord to stop construction on a porch he was adding to the house. I had made homemade doughnuts and the manager's wife said her husband loved doughnuts so I sent some home with her. I got a call back the next day with "many thanks-he ate them all!"

Meanwhile the house thing went on-Jim away, me desperate-I had heard that one of the service companies had a house that was vacant and they weren't planning to use it any time soon. "IDEA" They would be willing to rent it to Gulf and all it needed was the manager's approval! To make a long story short, I sent a poem pleading my case along with a dozen homemade doughnuts. I, after all, was holding an Art Show for Nigerian artists and that was a good "public relations effort" and a 2nd floor apartment would make it impossible to continue.

Well, who could refuse such a clever plea?! We got the house. Jim returned to find me ready to move into a much larger house with a screened in porch. He wasn't too happy with my negotiation skills but allowed how "they worked".

I converted the porch into a permanent shop. The Nigerian artists were very happy to be able to leave their artwork fulltime. I got many calls from visitors to Lagos to open shop so they could find something Nigerian to take back to the U.S.A. I finally had to have help, so I talked a friend into helping on Art Day and hired a man who could make frames for the many paintings we sold. I became an expert in color mats and frames out of necessity!

When we left Nigeria the newspaper sent out a reporter and she wrote a very nice article about me and my efforts to help Nigerian artists. I found someone to take over the job before we left and to carry on the tradition.

LAGOS NEWSPAPER ARTICLE

Newspaper article (verbatum) by Sereba Agiobu-Kemmer:

"For those who are artists and all those who belong to the artistic circle, the name Grace Black needs no introduction. For those who are not, however, so disposed, she is one woman, whose sympathy and efforts have gone a long way in assisting Nigerian artists to get the much desired patronage and exposure most of them lack. Artists cannot afford the time to go about seeking clients to buy their works as this would dissipate or sap their creative energies. Secondly most artists cannot afford to pay galleries to have their works displayed. And in any case, such galleries are too few.

Grace Black, apart from being an art lover and avid collector, had for the past four years, of her stay in this country devoted herself to helping, in a concrete way to solve one of the prime problems of Nigerian artist. At her home, she has a room turned permanently into a gallery and every Thursday, she holds an open house, where artists bring their works to show to invited guests who later became regular patrons. In this way, she has acted as the catalyst for both the artists and the society. Unfortunately she leaves soon for London which is the new posting of her husband, an employee of Gulf Oil Company. I notice their art collection includes pieces from different parts of the world such as countries in South America, the Carribbeans, Europe, Asia and Africa.

I was most impressed, by the Pre-Columbian art brass stirrups and leather-covered wooden chests from Venezuela, her African art which includes male and female chi-wara from the Bambara, a carved antique door from Bida and modern paintings of artists in Europe, and South America and many from Nigeria, from artists like Onabraepkeya, Dele Oshinowo, Oyelami, to mention a few, because her list includes over 28 Nigertian artists.

Her interest is such, that she has managed to convince another newcomer to carry on the work when she is gone. So there is no need to despair in that respect. Except that we shall miss such a quiet, but dynamic person in the art circle. I know many ladies, who would in addition miss their favourite bead-jewelry designer.

Although not claiming any professionalism, Grace Black, in her spare time, makes very original necklaces from African beads and paints mostly in pastel. She hopes to be able to arrange further exhibitions in London where she will be for the numerous Nigerian artists who have also become her personal friends.

This little tribute is to a very active friend of Nigerian artists. Also it is a tribute to her efforts which have made the weekly Thursday exhibition possible. It seems like a tradition has been set already. Before Grace there were persons, such as the Woolforth of the UN office in Lagos who started it all. Then Mr. and Mrs Schiff of the Ford foundation.

When they left, Mr. and Mrs Edwards of USAID took over. After them came the Fishe and their vivacious daughter Mimi, then it was the Coxs before the Blacks took over almost four years ago. But efforts will continue as Grace Black has managed to rub on some of her enthusiasm to a new comer Mrs. Madox who came in from Abidjan, just a few months ago, with her husband.

The Thursday exhibitions will now be held at their home. Over the years a patronising circle, has gradually been formed for the artists. As Grace Black, said, it is mostly made up of foreigners, although, they had witnessed some increase in the rather negligible number of Nigerians, she feels it, more desirable that Nigerians, themselves, should be more enthusiatic about their own art, at least enough, to patronise the artists. She sees no reason why Nigerian housewives cannot pick on the idea of organising such exhibitions, which she and many others have found to be most rewarding.

That is the challenge she throws out to the Nigerian public as she leaves this country with her husband and family to their next posting. So to the Blacks, it is goodbye and at the same time it is welcome to the Madoxs."

Lagos newspaper reporter and Nigeria farewell party

There were two nightclubs in Lagos and some good restaurants so we had plenty to do. There were golf courses and a movie once a week at the club. The Motor Boat Club 75 was a favorite place to go for good food although we usually put the coaster on top of the drink instead of under it-the flies were bad. One day the kids all came running back to the table crying for us to come look. There was a body floating in the water and no one seemed to be concerned.

Looking back we had a lot to contend with; our 4 ½ years were character building for sure. I had found a useful way to spend my time and developed my pastel technique well enough to sell several pastels. Jim got loads of experience managing difficult people. The girls all got their eyes opened to a real 3rd world country. Karen met her husband. John became a pretty self sufficient little boy and we made friends to last a lifetime.

COWBOY BOOTS

I must recount John's boot story. Remember those cowboy boots? Well, he finally grew into them, but by then they were pretty much worn out. Along came a cobbler to the door asking if we needed any shoes repaired. I gave him John's boots and he said he could make them like new.

About 2 months passed and I was pretty sure we weren't going to see those boots again. But back he came and sure enough they looked great. I put them in a corner so John would have a surprise when he returned from school. When he came home I pointed out the boots and he was elated.

That didn't last long-he kicked off his shoes, put his foot in one boot and out came dozens of roaches. He flung the boots across the room and we were both screaming and trying to do the roaches in. We finally sprayed them well and he had enough nerve to try again after we carefully examined them. He is now 40+ and says he never puts on an old pair of boots or shoes without checking them first.

While in Nigeria Claire graduated from 9th grade and we were going to check on boarding schools on our vacation. There were several in Europe and one in Tangiers. On our way to check schools for Claire we stopped off in the Ivory Coast. Nothing stands out in particular except it seemed very clean after Nigeria. It had been a French colony, so a lot of French influence. The French intermarried with the native peoples and all seemed well integrated.

We went on to Morocco-a completely different place for Africa. We stayed in Casablanca, didn't see Rick, but went to the hotel where Somerset Maugham stayed. We went to the market place and were surrounded by little boys wanting to be our "guide". After saying "no" to many of them we finally decided to hire one to keep the others away. There were all kinds of sights; snake charmers, and many things for sale. We went into the Souk and were mildly interested in a small rug. We were treated like royalty; sat down on cushions and served tea! Then the vendors pulled down myriads of rugs and we kept saying, "No, we just want to look and, maybe buy a small one". By the end of an hour we had purchased a 12x14 beautiful white wool rug with a brown Indian design. We paid for it and went on our way. We wanted it sent to London where we had our other things in storage. NO PROBLEM. After we left we figured we would never see it again and we would be out that money, but our sales resistance had been completely shattered. It did arrive in London, much to our amazement!

We somehow heard of a school in Austria. It was run by an American couple. That was to be our first stop. We flew into Salzburg, saw some of the town, the Lippizaner horse show, the Vienna Boy's Choir and made our way to the small town of Faistenau. It was a very small Austrian village. We spoke to the principal of the school and toured around the town. It was a beautiful setting and we all expected Julie Andrews to appear any minute and sing Edelweiss. We made arrangements then and there. Claire was sure she wanted to stay there for school. She did well there completing 3 years of high school in 2 and entered Roanoke College a year early.

We were on vacation and Claire would be staying with my brother. He volunteered to take her to school in Roanoke, VA, and I headed back to Nigeria to join Jim who went ahead of us. Somehow our passports got switched in the shuffle of last minute plans. John and I traveled to New York. I handed my passports to the official and lo-and-behold there was Claire's face looking up at me! What to do now? I immediately called my brother and arranged for him to send my passport "overnight mail". John and I got a hotel room, changed our reservations, sent a telegram to Jim that we were "delayed" and waited in hopes my passport would arrive. I was a nervous wreck by the time we finally boarded our plane with my passport in hand. We stopped in Haiti to change planes and John kept his eye on the plane the whole time worrying that we might miss the plane and never get back home. We did and believe it or not, Nigeria and home looked pretty good by then.

So, the beginning of the next year left us with only John at home.

ANOTHER SHIP DIDN'T COME IN

Karen and Bengt came back to Nigeria with my first grandchild, Ryan Alexander. Bengt had secured a good job With Uncle Ben's Rice. It was really great having them close. Bengt decided to go into business himself transporting rice into Nigeria. He had a business partner, Dr Hassan, and he was sent to Thailand to load a ship with rice which he did. When he got back they waited for the ship to arrive and it never did, so Bengt's ship didn't come in a second time. One rumor had it that Hassan rerouted the ship. They left Lagos and were to go to California where Bengt had some contacts.

"WHAT COLOR DRESS"

Susan called from Florida. She was planning to get married. I had met the young man on a previous visit and wasn't impressed but I was learning my lesson about objections, so I decided to keep quiet on this one "NOT EASY". She wanted to know what color dress I might choose for the wedding-Mrs G was wearing blue. My answer was, "I'm wearing BLACK". And she said, "OH MOM". Maybe the thought of her mom arriving in black gave her second thoughts-anyway she called off the wedding-and I breathed a huge sigh of relief.

LAGOS FAREWELL

If you are a student of poetry
And enjoy a rhyme or two,
Please overlook my irregular style
For this poem is meant for you.

To say goodbye is not our way
For we'd rather say "See you again one day".
For looking over the last four years
The friends we've made, the laughter and tears
Have been worth more than we can possibly say
And we'll no doubt wish we were back one day.
The many Sundays we've spent at the beach,
The friends we phoned but couldn't reach,
The friendly bridge games, the kind words spoken
The volley ball games-Victor's leg broken
The fourth of July, and the P.T.A.
The flood on Awolowa, it rained that day
The arrival of new faces and old friends too
The departure of friends that made us blue
The excitement of Festac coming to town
The bridges being built, the new roads going round
The anguish of traffic and the new road laws
And the difficulty remembering what day it was
The crowded city and the walks being paved
The beautiful beach where the palm trees swayed
The power cuts soothed by the balmy breezes
With the water running out and the melting deepfreezes
The boat that we couldn't keep the water out
The joy of the new one speeding about
We've balanced it all out-we've weighed the good and the bad
The weeks in and the weeks out and some hard times we've had
And we thought you'd like to know 'cause there's a lot of truth in it
Remember it when you think you've reached your limit
That learning to know your fellow man
Living the good days and bad as best you can
Loving your friends-Nigerians, Oakies and even Yankees-without a doubt
Is really what life is all about.

    The Blacks

All good things must come to an end. We got word that we would be moving to London.
I thought I had died and gone to Heaven.

LONDON TOWN

Our arrival in London was in plenty of time to register John in school; The American School of London.

We were assigned a small company apartment and stayed there a couple of months. We finally moved to another apartment in Swiss Cottage, a suburb of London. We were informed that one could rent or buy depending on pay scale. I looked at many apartments and was having trouble finding a decent one. Most were in different modes of disrepair. Jim was travelling back and forth to Norway to set up an office there, so he was gone a lot.

The company apartment was furnished with bare essentials-the refrigerator was the smallest I'd ever seen. It seemed that the whole place was meant for Liliputions.

Our foray into the grocery store was a disaster. We bought what we thought would be a starter amount of food and supplies and at the check-out counter we were given gallon size bags. We discovered that most Brits only bought groceries on a day-to-day basis and brought their own carts. John and I stood watch over our bags while Jim made numerous trips back to the car with the 40+ bags. I'm sure the locals thought we were crazy Americans! After getting used to the system I made out quite well. It wasn't what I expected back in civilization.

Before finding an apartment they decided to send us to Norway. As the old saying goes, "All good things must come to an end". Jim had been there many times and assured me I would love it, HMM!

SUMMER VACATION IN IRELAND

Before going to Norway we were to spend a summer in Ireland. Claire and John went with us and Jim was in charge of an offshore well. We stayed in Limerick and had a wonderful summer. I fell in love with the Irish People and still find Irishmen full of the old blarney-but fascinating! Someone said the Lord invented liquor so the Irish wouldn't rule the world! We started out in Dublin and Claire and I ate strawberries and cream till we couldn't hold anymore.

We made a preliminary trip to Norway at Christmas time. The town was Stavanger, a small port town on a fiord, very beautifully decorated for the holidays-the shops and streets were delightful.

We found a house right away. It was a new house, an A-frame situated right on a fiord. We cleaned up the house in London and off we went to Stavanger.

John wasn't too happy about leaving London either. The school was good, they had a good boy's soccer team and that helped. We took him to the American School in Norway to register and he seemed happy there.

The Norwegian language is difficult-it took me 2 weeks to pronounce the name of street we lived on. Most of the people spoke English so we were able to get by nicely.

Jim had spent a lot of time finding office space and hiring personnel but after we were settled Gulf brought in a geologist to be the manager. It was a couple we knew in Nigeria. The man, a very hard worker, smoked like a steam engine and his wife, a rather salty woman. They had 2 children. Jim didn't seem to mind and suggested that since they were having a little trouble finding a big enough house maybe we should offer them the one we found-my answer, "Over my dead body".

Life in Norway was pleasant. The climate was cold but very little snow. The people were great and couldn't do enough to help us. We did have one snow and we all tried our skills at cross country skiing.

The Norwegians had a reputation for being heavy drinkers and we were told if you have a party only put out what you plan to serve because no one will leave until all is gone. The drinking and driving penalties were very stiff and usually involved jail time. The taxis all did a good business. Liquor was expensive and most locals made their own.

One evening we attended a party at a local restaurant and it was very crowded. Many were at the bar and I was seated in a chair along the wall. To my surprise a big man came over and sat on my lap. He was helped off by the man next to me saying. "Don't think anything about it, he's a Laplander".

We were invited to a party at a friend's home and needed a baby sitter for John. The manager's daughter was hired. When we got home we asked John if everything went OK. He said. "I guess so. She said if you don't behave I'll knock the s—out of you". Many years later we heard that she was a police officer in California and had won many awards!

While there, we were all invited to tour one of the huge offshore semi submersible drilling rigs that were being built on the fiord. We went out to it by boat and jumped from the boat to an open ladder. It was a little over my expertise-but I made it. I couldn't enjoy the tour wondering how I would make it back to the boat-I did!

Barbara joined us and got a job with Gulf. Claire came for the summer and worked there too. So they both got some experience in the ways of an oil company.

We were there for about 8 months when Jim had to travel to Gabon in West Africa. The girls had all gone back to the States and I was to stay 2 months till Christmas and meet him in the States for Susan's wedding. She had met a great guy she was sure I would love (I did), Duncan Harding.

Karen, Bengt and Ryan came for a visit and went to Sweden to meet Bengt's family. Ryan, a spunky little 2-year old, was the center of attention!

I was alone with John who came home from school late and went to bed-it got dark at 2:30 PM. No TV and a howling wind. I lasted 2 weeks. I sent a letter to Jim. "I'm out of here. See you in Florida".

We found a small private school for John, he did very well there and I was able to help plan Susan's wedding. Susan and Duncan were married at Jean's (Jim's sister) church. It was a small wedding. All 4 parents were there but it rained cats and dogs. Susan had found a great guy. Their marriage lasted 30 years until her death in 2008 of breast cancer.

We went back to Norway after vacation and guess what? They wanted Jim back in London. We used part of that vacation to go on a Norwegian Cruise ship and toured the Greek islands with Claire and John.

Our deal with the landlord was to leave our kitchen appliances plus the washer and dryer. He was thrilled to get them. One thing we noticed in Norway was a lot of bartering was going on. The exchange of work-no money was involved if it was under the table. All this was to avoid the huge taxes. The people were happy with free education and medical but thought up all sorts of ways to avoid taxes. So this is Socialism-makes everyone a lawbreaker.

Barb had to give up her job and decided to go to London with us and attend secretary school. Claire went back to Colorado College where she had transferred her sophomore year.

I wasn't too upset about returning to London. We hated to leave Norway and our house on the fiord but duty called and we were on our way.

LONDON TOWN AGAIN

As soon as we arrived, we went back to reregister John at the American School of London. We were thrilled to find our old friends Ernie and Mollie Haynes already there. Their son, Matt, was John's age and they both loved soccer. One of the highlights of John's and Matt's soccer careers was winning a soccer game at an English school playing in the mud and rain. No small accomplishment for a bunch of American kids!

I on the other hand was going through the exhausting job of finding a house or apartment and after daily trips with an agent and looking for over a month we caught wind of a vacant apartment that had belonged to a Gulf employee who had been transferred. It was a little over our budget in the loan department but Jim worked out a deal to buy it and when it sold we would give Gulf 30% of the profit. There was a really good market at that time and many people made huge profits when they sold. We figured it was a pretty good investment besides I was exhausted trying to find a decent place to live.

London Apartment

It was a great apartment within walking distance to the school, shopping on High Street and Jim could even walk to work.

Living in London was as wonderful as I remembered. Our next door neighbors were Dolly and Jim Ferrell. Dolly and I became good friends and made many trips to Rochester to buy china. Dolly already had every space filled with her purchases there, but never turned down a trip to look for a "special buy". It was like the china demon was after us. Dolly was much braver than I. She took up driving and we drove all over town on the left side of the road, steering wheel on the wrong side-I never made it. I took one spin around the block in my car and my passenger nearly had a heart attack.

THE IMARI CHINA

I was able to buy my beautiful Imari Royal Crown Derby china while in London and it is one of my prize possessions. It only comes to the table on special occasions-mostly at Christmas. The family has always made a big joke out of my warnings that no one should try to wash it after dinner is over. I am the only one allowed to do that. My oldest grandson always makes a big production of carrying his plate to the kitchen warning all of the rest of the family that to break a plate would mean instant death or at least banishment from the family. So, since he was the first to marry, I wrote a little poem leaving the china to him in the hopes that he will divide it up with the rest of the kids at the proper time. Maybe they can set a place at Christmas for Grandma!

The famous china!

UNIVERSITY OF LONDON

I joined a group of women in a University of London course on English history. We went twice a week to most of the historical areas in London, took notes and then had lunch together. Our guide was a great old man (around 70+) who could out walk and out talk a much younger group. We all thoroughly enjoyed the course. I found a group of ladies to play bridge.

We joined the American Church of London which was held at Whitefield Church named for George Whitefield one of the founders of Methodism. We became quite active in the church. There were many Americans in London who attended there and we met people from all walks of life. Our minister who was loved by all decided to retire and a search was on for a new minister to take his place. A very nice retired military chaplain came with his wife and the congregation decided to hire him. His wife was to return to the U.S. and then come back to London when one of their children was out of school. She came to spend Christmas and all seemed well. After the first of the year a new member joined the church. She was single, attractive, redhead and became very active in the church. We all wondered how she managed to be without a job due to very strict British laws on work permits.

During this time while talking to the minister I discovered he had a daughter attending the Air Force Academy. I suggested he give me her name and phone # and my daughter who lived in Colorado Springs would call her. After that conversation he avoided me at every turn and I couldn't figure out what was going on. Soon we learned that his wife wouldn't be joining him and that the red haired lady was "the other woman". When this news broke he was promptly let go for deceiving the congregation and we finally hired another minister.

That Thanksgiving we participated in the service at Westminster Cathedral and that was a very memorable event.

THANKSGIVING PRAYER

Dear Lord:
On this
Thanksgiving Day we offer up a prayer
To thank you for giving us a lot more than our share.
So often we accept these things without thanks or praise
The many blessings you send us in so very many ways.
Help us Lord to remember that the joy of life and living
Is to make our prayers a prayer of thanks and every day
THANKSGIVING.

Claire and Mike were married this year, 1980, in Colorado Springs. Mike was the assistant hockey coach at Colorado College and became head coach, hence two sons who excelled in hockey. The whole family headed for Colorado and rented an apartment for a week. Claire had everything planned to a T and had chosen a beautiful antique lace dress. The first occasion was a dinner held by Mike's parents. On touring Old Colorado City we wandered into a cowboy store and decided it would be a great idea for the whole family to buy red and black checked western shirts for the party. I'm sure the Bertsch family thought we were all crazy or were a band and going to start playing music for the party. All went well and Claire and Mike were married in Shove Chapel at Colorado College. We all headed back with our cowboy shirts that hung in the closet for many years!

After Claire graduated from Colorado College we drove up the mountain to Woodland Park. I was so impressed I thought I might buy a nice vacation house or a lot there. Little did I know that later I'd still be there the rest of my days.

THE DREAM HOUSE IN WOODLAND PARK

The surroundings reminded me of an area we found while touring Pennsylvania. We happened on a new housing development that was located in a rural area with lots of trees and several A-frame homes-deer grazing in the yards. I was tempted to buy a lot there but better judgment prevailed since we didn't even know if we would come back to PA to live.

So, while on a short trip to Colorado for a business meeting in Durango, I left Jim to come to Colorado Springs to see Claire and Mike. Claire had a good friend who was in real estate for the area and I decided I'd come up to Woodland Park to maybe buy a cabin or a lot to build on later. After looking for several days and not finding anything I liked, the agent said, "I know of a house that is for sale by owner would you like to look at it?" I really wasn't interested in a house but agreed to have a look-we drove up the driveway and there it was, a lovely A-frame house nestled among aspen and evergreens next to the National Forrest and there was a deer grazing in the yard. Well, I hardly even needed to see the inside-it was perfect!

The owner made me a deal and I called Jim and told him to come to Colorado Springs as soon as he was finished with his meeting saying, "I think I've found the house of my dreams." When he arrived he liked it too and we bought it immediately. Claire and Mike took care of the closing and we were now the owners of our home in the mountains.

The dream house

OUR CHRISTMAS BLESSING

Friends and family make Christmas day
With carols sung in the same old way.
The giving of gifts to those we love,
As a reminder of the gift from God above.
In a manger in Bethlehem Jesus was born
And a star shone bright that Christmas morn.
To celebrate his birthday he, born in a stable,
Brings love to us and to our table.

Claire, Mike, Susan and Duncan came to London for Christmas and Jim was able to set up a pheasant hunt for the men. It was an experience they would never forget. I had a great time showing off wonderful London to them.

THE SPORT OF KINGS

Jim, John and I had been on several shoots; one to a Scottish castle, and one to an English castle, Arundel, home of the Duke of Norfolk, sponsored by Macobar. There was a photographer who took photos of every move we made. We were sent an album of all of the photos and it became Jim's favorite possession. During some of the shoots the English custom was to stop at mid morning and serve fruit cake and sloe gin. That was a first for all of the American Hunters! John was able to accompany us to Wales where we stayed at Ruthin Castle Hotel an authentic castle that was renovated and opened as a hotel.

Ernie and Molly were transferred to Scotland and we joined them for Thanksgiving. Ernie had found a small castle called Forbes Castle and they were living there on a temporary basis. Ernie said it cost $300 a month to heat and that was in the summer. We had a great time. The men went on a pheasant shoot so we had a pheasant Thanksgiving dinner. It was a week we would never forget. The scenery was so beautiful. The castle though small was still furnished with most of the original furniture. Portraits of the family descendants lined the winding staircase. The dining room table was large enough to seat 25. Our bedrooms and bath were pretty old fashioned but comfortable. The turret was filled with trunks and they had old clothing of days past. The kids had a great time going through them but were warned to replace everything back as found.

Ernie and Mollie's Forbes Castle in Scotland and Ruthin Castle in Wales

WHY DID OUR ANCESTERS LEAVE?

Later that year Ernie and Mollie renovated the large entertainment room with Scottish plaid curtains, good Scotch whiskey and were hosts to L. B. Johnson on his trip to Scotland.

Jim and Ernie were standing one day at the front door of the castle surveying the scene and Jim said, "You know my ancestors came from Scotland-it's so beautiful here I wonder why they ever left". Ernie in his usual sardonic humor said, "Probably because they were the beaters, not the shooters". Beaters being the Lower Class caretakers who, when the master of the estate came to shoot pheasants, would beat the bushes with sticks so the pheasants would fly!

Harrods, London's well known department store, was almost a tourist attraction. It was a department store and a food store. The food store was typically "Old English" and had chickens and turkeys hanging by the neck waiting to be chosen. (Maury says the way the French, English and American gourmet bird eaters determined if their bird was aged sufficiently would be to let the bird hang by his neck until the neck parted from its body- the meat may be a bit smelly but tender.) Once a year they had a huge china sale and you could find the most elegant china stacked up on tables where you had to move things around if you saw a pattern you liked.

LONDON VIGNETTES

Our apartment was within walking distance from Jim's office and we used the underground for most of our soirees into town and mostly used the famous London taxis when the underground wasn't running. The London taxi drivers were a source of entertainment and were experts on just about every subject, local or international. I remember a discourse when the price of gas went up very high and I was a passenger coming in from the airport. The taxi driver was ranting and raving about the oil companies. He asked where I was coming from and when he asked if I was with the embassy, I meekly said, "Yes!"

One exciting occasion while we were there was the Royal Wedding. It was to take place July 29 (Jim's and my anniversary). We watched all of the wedding and the beautiful royal pageantry and we thought it was perfect.

Ernie and Mollie had a big party that night. Their apartment was on the other side of town. Upon leaving we found the underground closed and no taxis to be found. We walked most of the way home but finally found a taxi by entering a hotel staying a short while and then coming out and having the doorman secure a taxi. (an old Londoner's trick; it worked like a charm.)

Years later looking back it was all make believe-the ruination of a sweet young thing-a true princess Diana turned into a beautiful woman but was degraded by the life chosen for her by her prince who turned out to be a frog! Her death, years later, was such a tragedy and we felt sorrow as though we had known her personally. I watched her son marry in 2011 and hope he is cut of better cloth.

Barbara came to London with us and decided to take a secretarial course while there. The school was located within the heart of London on Bond Street. One day while walking to school, she encountered Dustin Hoffman. She was so flustered that instead of asking for his autograph, she said, "Would you sign an autograph for my sister?" He asked her name, "Barbara" she said and he wrote the autograph, "To Barbara." We all got a big laugh out of that tale.

There were so many foreigners in London that the joke was if you were walking down Oxford Street and saw an Englishman you would ask, "Dr Livingstone, I presume"?

One evening while on our way to the famous German restaurant, Luchows, we stopped to listen at Speaker's Corner (a place allocated for anyone to spout their political views or any other subject they wished). One man there on his soap box was touting the tenants of Communism. Jim got so agitated he was about to argue with him and I pulled him away just before a confrontation. There were two big guys standing beside the speaker who looked like bodyguards. Jim grumbled all through dinner at the injustice of the occasion.

JR IS COMING TO TOWN

While we were in London, Ernie and Mollie informed us that Larry Hagman was coming to town and they were going to throw a big cocktail party for him. During that time "Dallas" was a big favorite with the Brits, so there was an air of excitement in the land. They had been in touch with Ernie's sister, Ann Hodges, was the TV editor for the Houston Chronical newspaper and was a personal friend of Larry.

There was a clamoring for invitations to this affair and we were invited. The big evening arrived and there he was, J.R. himself! He was very charming and everyone came away thinking he was one of the nice guys from Hollywood. He had just stopped smoking and carried around a small fan in case the errant smoker was talking to him the smoke would blow back at the smoker. We had a great conversation with Larry and luckily we didn't smoke! The party was a big success. He later invited Ernie and Mollie to his home in California in appreciation of their hospitality.

JR and friends

I decided to go to California to see Karen and little Ryan. When I arrived she was very distraught. They were living in a very small apartment, she had a job, Bengt was looking for work but drinking a lot. The fridge was bare and Karen had just had her jewelry stolen-mostly gifts we had given her through the years for special occasions. When I left to go back to London I left her a ticket and told her she could come when and if things got worse. She and Ryan arrived several weeks later. The idea was to give Bengt a chance to get back on his feet again and realize that California wasn't the golden opportunity for everyone.

After several months she went back to Orlando and stayed with Susan and Duncan. We arrived back on vacation and she was desperately looking for a job. I was helping her by scouring the want ads. I came across an ad and we decided it looked interesting. She called for an interview and I went with her. It was the start up of a new concept in vacations called 'Time Share'. The name of the company was 'Vistana' and their office was in a trailer-not too impressive. We were shown the unit which they had remodeled-it was very nice and we both thought it was a clever idea. Karen was hired on the spot and even convinced them she would need several weeks to travel to London before starting. This began her successful career.

It turned out our assessment of the vacation time share really took off-especially in Orlando where Disney had a firm hold. The small beginning of Vistana has grown today to many units, world class tennis courts and several pools. Karen was in on the ground floor and made a very good living for herself and Ryan through the years. She became one of their top salespersons and was eventually in management. She lured Susan from her nursing career and Susan did well there too. Karen bought a small house. Bengt's behavior didn't improve and we were there when he left the picture-a divorce finalized.

We bought a home in Orlando and rented it with the idea we would retire there but Colorado and Claire kept pulling us back to the mountains. Several years later when Claire graduated we were there and then back again for her wedding.

IT CAN'T GET ANY BETTER THAN THIS-BUT

Jim came home one day and had a strange look on his face. He was needed in Indonesia!! I wasn't too enthusiastic to say the least. I felt we were finally in our proper place in life and were ready to retire there in several years. John was happy and the American School of London seemed the perfect place for him.

After dragging my feet for as long as I could I had to accept the inevitable so we prepared to leave London. I managed to talk Jim into us staying until John finished the school year. That left me with the task of moving, closing on the apartment and get permits for Jim's guns. By that time the housing market was down and we didn't make much on the sale of the apartment. Jim said, "Well that fits our pattern-buy high, sell low".

Our arrival in Jakarta was put off for a few days because it was the Chinese New Year, so we stopped in Singapore where we met the company rep who told us about the house we had waiting and what to expect of life in Jakarta.

When we finally arrived there the house we were assigned was beautiful, manicured, oriental garden with a fish pond, a huge living area, servant's quarters and orchids growing in the front yard. We stayed in the hotel until our furniture arrived.

The first thing to do was enroll John in school. He was feeling rather out of sorts about another new school but when he arrived there someone yelled out, "Hey John Black". It was a former classmate from Norway. He was a junior in high school by then and started playing soccer right away. So the transition was painless again. He took on coaching the girl's soccer team and that proved to be a great pastime for a teenage boy!

Our first night in our new home was a little unusual. In the middle of the night we heard a big commotion. We got up and searched the grounds, the maid's quarters and finally realized it was the call to worship being broadcast from the nearby mosque. We finally got used to it and seldom heard it again.

Entrance to house in Jakarta

I went about the task of making draperies from the beautiful BATIK materials available. I hired a sewing lady who said she could make slip covers for my old sofa. She didn't want to use my machine so she brought a small one of her own and sat on the floor sewing up a storm- the covers turned out perfectly.

We were off to a good start but the first time we left the house thieves came in and carried off our stereo equipment and TV in broad daylight. The maid neither saw nor heard anything. We had a nice group with Gulf and some we knew from countries past. We purchased a saltwater aquarium and filled it with all kinds of fish and anemones. We placed it between the dining and living rooms and set up a bar with a Kelly green background wall where I hung my zebra skin. It turned out to be one of our nicest houses.

As usual we were met by old friends from different places in our journeys. The Buzardes who were with Gulf in Nigeria were there when we arrived. He was now the manager of IAPCO. Buzz asked Jim's advice about making the move to Jakarta and leaving his job with Gulf. Jim said, "Go for it". We were very pleased to find Buzz at the top of the ladder when we arrived in Jakarta.

Our old friend, Maury Hammond, showed up-seems like we just kept meeting each other along the way. He stayed in our house while we were on vacation. Big Blue, our favorite aquarium fish, expired on his watch and the houseboy greeted us with, "Mr Hammond killed BIG BLUE". We never let him live that down.

Life in Jakarta was much better than I hoped. The Indonesian people were very gifted in the arts. Their music played, on the gamelan (a mixture of percussion instruments (gongs, etc)), was charmingly unusual. They made beautiful flower arrangements and ice sculptures.

Gamelon musicians in Jakarta

Ristoffel is served at Jakarta Hilton

One of the popular items to acquire was a "gong", a large brass melodious gong usually mounted on a wooden stand. We made the trip to the factory to order one. I still use it to call "dinner time" or "play bridge".

The BATIK material made by people old and young working on a dirt floor from morning to night was unbelievably beautiful but seeing how it was made took the joy out of it for me.

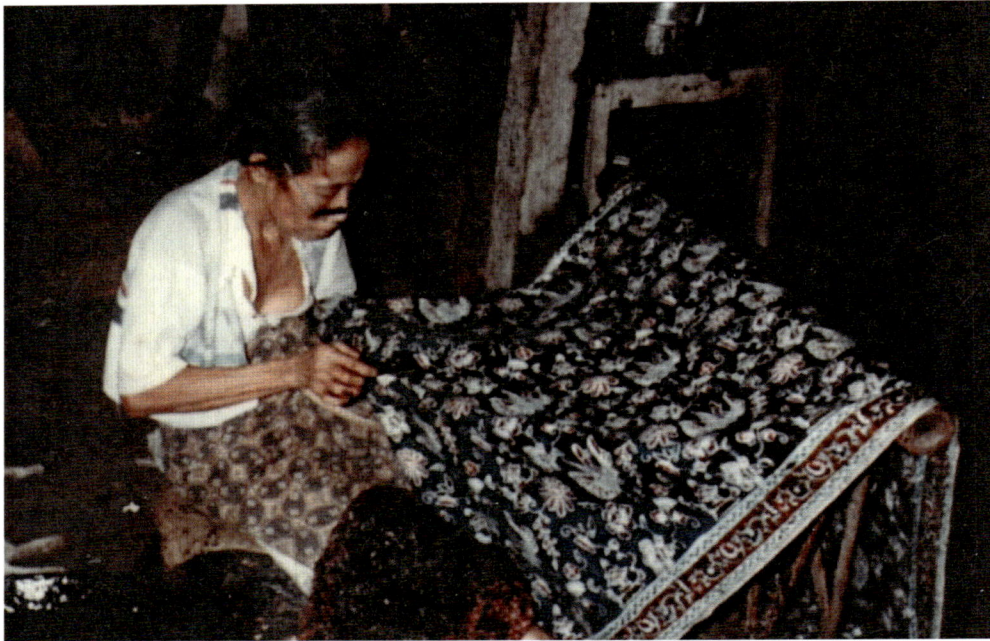
Batik lady in Jakarta

There were many antique shops in town and I scoured all of them hoping to find a treasure. My treasure was a beautiful carved Chinese bed. It made it all the way back to Woodland Park and is a conversation piece in a corner of my bedroom-I might also add that it's a prize cobweb catcher.

Chinese bed and vendors

We also found old Chinese pottery, inlaid chests with mother of pearl and gold embroidered ceremonial sarongs worn at weddings by the bride and groom.

Indonesia was by far the most interesting place we ever lived. The people were friendly and courteous and their art and customs so different.

My apprehension at leaving London was all unfounded. We have been asked by many people, "Which country did you like best (this was our 8th) or would you like to go back to?" Indonesia rated at the top of the list.

In today's world most of the places we lived are HOT SPOTS for tourists and are under the rule of communism or violent Muslims. Chavez and his ilk in Venezuela are ruining the great country we called home for 17 years. It is so discouraging to realize all of the efforts and hardships we endured going to waste. Not only our efforts for the U.S. but for the local people; jobs, education and a healthy life seem to have gone unnoticed by the new regimes. Most of the leaders in the oil industry and other industries were educated in the U.S. paid for by the oil companies.

CHERRY BLOSSOMS AND GEISHAS

Grace and John in Tokyo

We made a trip to Japan while in Indonesia. We arrived during Cherry Blossom time. It was one of the most beautiful sights I have ever seen. The whole population were enjoying the time and were sitting in parks with picnic baskets and walking through the wonderland of nature.

We were invited to a dinner served by Geishas-quite an experience. I got to try on a fantastic KIMONO and still have a picture taken in this elegant outfit. All in all it was a perfect glimpse into a life of times past.

The new generation was busy rushing about with their phones and music players. The taxi drivers are left over KAMIKASI pilots and the trains were fantastic. We went back to Indonesia with a new appreciation of oriental culture.

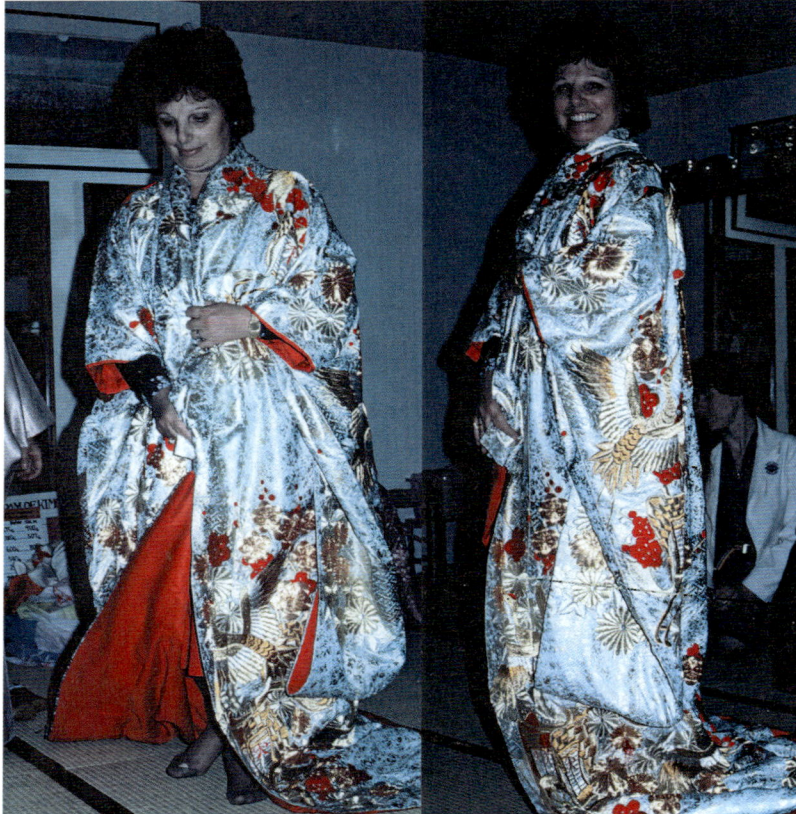

American geisha

We also made a trip to Sydney Australia and what a great place that was. We felt very lucky to have had the opportunity to visit these places.

I was approaching my 50th birthday and was in the States for a short vacation with John. We were headed back via Thailand and Jim was to meet us there. At the airport the taxi driver said we would take a short cut to the hotel. On the way we had a torrential rain, the car got stuck on a dirt road and the water was up to the doors. We thought we were goners. The car was soon surrounded by people and they literally pushed us to safety. We finally got to the hotel and I was sure when we opened the trunk our luggage would float out but for some strange reason all was dry.

We spent several days there shopping and sightseeing. It was depressing to see the poverty of the people living along the river in small huts. They all waved happily as we went by and seemed to be content with their surroundings.

BALI HIGH

We arrived back to Jakarta and took several trips while there to Bali. On one trip we were to meet Maury Hammond at the Bali Beach Hotel. Turned out there were several BBHs. Maury looked in all of them and was about to give up and go to the airport to catch a flight back to Jakarta when he spotted a tall person down the street a foot or so above the Balinese-it was Jim. He waited until we were all seated in a restaurant and came up behind Jim and gave Jim hell for sending him on a wild goose chase. Maury calmed down somewhat when Jim escorted him down to a beach where most of the women were topless. I might add there were naked men too-our men pronounced them disgusting. The tables were turned.

MONKEY BUSINESS

On this trip we went to see the monkeys. Not a good experience. When we arrived all the monkeys were running loose trying to jump on us looking for food; sometimes spraying you with urine. Needless to say that's one place I wouldn't revisit or recommend.

INTO THE DEEP

Maury had a friend there who had invited us to his house for drinks before dinner. It was a lovely BALI home and his girlfriend, a very attractive Chinese girl was there to greet us. We all had several drinks and were ready to leave at dark. Maury's friend said, "I'm sorry but my outside lights aren't working. When you come to the bridge-it's over a small stream-sort of a drainage ditch. So be careful." It was so dark you couldn't see your hand in front of your face. I was groping my way along, took one step and fell into the water. The rest of the party couldn't see me. Jim yelled, "Are you OK?" My reply, "No, I'm all wet!"

They finally got me fished out and we went back to the house. I, dripping wet, and the others showing 'mild concern' but barely able to keep straight faces. The little size 6 Chinese girl said, "I'll get you some dry clothes". I told her I doubted I'd fit into anything she had. Soon she brought out a moo-moo type dress she had bought for her aunt and a pair of panties which on me were more like a G string.

We finally made it out on the second try and everyone was ready to have dinner. I said, "No way I'm going like this" so they went on and I went back to the hotel to change. Everyone had a good laugh when I arrived looking like a drowned rat-my hair do ruined and my pride injured. But by that time I was able to see the humor in the incident.

DON'T BELIEVE IT

Word came that the big bosses were to plan a cocktail party and an excursion for the wives. It all went well and Gulf employees quizzed the exec about rumors that were going around that Gulf Oil was going to be sold. They assured us that this wasn't so. Several months later it was official. Gulf was sold to Chevron Oil Company and now we all waited to hear what that would mean to us. The word came that we would all be going back to Houston to get our assignments. In the meantime we sent John back to stay with Claire and Mike to finish his last year of high school. Poor John-moved again.

Jim asked the Gulf president if he could take early retirement and that was finally granted. We were given a great send off; a big party for the general public and a nice office party. Jim was given a beautiful brass tray showing a map of Indonesia. I was given a beautiful ceremonial sarong. I gave one of my pastels to his faithful secretary. It was a scene from a Texas' countryside with a cottage and bluebonnets. The next step was to sell most of our furniture and household items.

Goodbye Jakarta

We were overdue to take a vacation and were at odds as to what to which route to take back to the States. Jim wanted to go to New Zealand and I wanted to go on an African photo safari which had been my dream for many years. We had some sort of a bet-I don't even remember what is was now, but I won and we were off to East Africa. John was home on vacation so he was able to accompany us.

Our flight took us via Singapore where we stopped off for a few nights and bought a really good camera for the trip.

OFF TO NAIROBI AT LAST

Our second stop was the Seychelles Islands here we spent 2 days. The beaches were wonderful and the big attraction was wind surfing. I couldn't get up enough nerve to try but we spent the day watching take-offs and landings.

We finally arrived in Nairobi where we joined a safari tour of Kenya. We went by van over the Serengeti viewing all of the animals of Africa. We stayed the night at Tree Tops where Queen Elizabeth got the news she had become queen. We visited a Maasai village and on to see the amazing countryside of East Africa. It was the trip of a lifetime. We took many pictures and came so close to the animals that we didn't need the telescope. Jim conceded that the trip was well worth his missing out on New Zealand and he enjoyed it as much as I. I always felt remorse that he never got to New Zealand. We stopped off in London on our way to Houston. I had my hair done by my old hairdresser-it was almost like coming home.

With Maasai Headhunters

Maasai girl wearing her jewels

Treetops

Kenyan Natives

We arrived home and found that Jim's request for early retirement was granted. It was 1985.

NOW WHAT?

We no longer had Father Gulf to tell us where to go! We decided to go to Orlando to try to make up our minds. We still had our house there in which Susan and Duncan were living. We moved in with Susan and Duncan and tried to decide our next move.

Barbara was married in 1986 to Nelson Betancourt just after we retired from Gulf. Karen and Susan helped plan her wedding since we weren't able to be in Orlando at that time.

It was a beautiful garden wedding and most of the family were able to attend. Karen and Susan playing the good sisters worked like crazy to get it all together-they said they might need a rest home when it was all over. Neither of them had a daughter so it was a good life experience for them. I waltzed in at the last moment and played the grand dame! Jim was handsome in his tux and Ryan carried the ring.

Orlando had changed. We had spent vacations there over the years. Disney had taken over the small sleepy town and it was now a bustling city with all kinds of "Worlds" and lots of traffic. We went back and forth from Colorado to Orlando for almost 2 years and when our shipment came we had it sent to Woodland Park since our house there had a huge garage that would store our "THINGS" until we decided on our next plan.

Every time we stayed there we opened a few more boxes and finally when almost everything was unpacked, Woodland Park became our permanent home. The Orlando kids weren't too happy with our decision. They said it was the kids who were supposed to leave home!

MOVE TO THE MOUNTAINS

Claire and Mike were living in Colorado Springs and had a beautiful baby boy, Sean. They decided to move to Woodland Park and started the process of finding a house or a lot to build on. No hurry, though, they had to sell their house and that would take time. Not so! It sold almost immediately and while driving around Woodland Park, Jim and I found a beautiful area with new lots for sale. They decided to build their home there and their view of Pikes Peak is still unsurpassed in the Woodland Park area. We went back to Florida and they stayed in our house till theirs was finished. When their house was finished, we moved back to Woodland Park permanently. Chinese bed and all!

During this time, Claire was expecting a new baby and was having back problems. I went with her to a medical supply store where she was to pick up a special back support. Sean and I waited in the car and she took forever. Sean was getting pretty antsy and so to keep him entertained, I noticed an American flag flying nearby and proceeded to teach him The Star Spangled Banner. By the time Claire came back, Sean and I were happily singing The Star Spangled Banner and he knew it all by heart.

He astounded Ernie and Mollie when they visited. He was 3 years old and before starting his toy hockey game, we all had to stand and sing The Star Spangled Banner. Sean of course was introduced to hockey from the womb. He has had quite a career playing hockey with the Air Force Academy and is the pride of his grandmother.

AISLINN

Barbara and Nelson's daughter, Aislinn, was born in 1990. We were planning a trip to the Keys when Aislinn decided it was time to enter this world. Part of the family went on to the Keys and we stayed with Barb till Aislinn arrived, a beautiful Latina-Nelson was half Columbian and she today takes after his side of the family in looks.

POP UP-FILLED UP

We bought a pop-up camper and took many vacations together and when Jessie arrived, we had a car full! And a camper full. Little did we know that we could fit in two more little ones. Cara was born next and then Jared. The last two were so close together that when Jim heard of Jared's impending arrival, he stood up and paced back and forth saying, "I just don't know what we'll do"! That got a big laugh from all of us. What we did was welcome Jared into the family with delight and he's still entertaining us to this day!

We had many happy trips; playing games in the car, 20 Questions, counting the next group of antelope and singing, "Home on the range". Sean always added, "Where the deer and the antelope play and it doesn't rain all day".

John was in college at Kilgore, Texas, and Susan and Duncan decided to move to Colorado. After looking at many houses and lots we decided to deed 1 acre of our land so they could build a small log house close to us. Just a little house among the trees. I stressed that I didn't want their house to be seen even from my window. All went well, the plans pleased everyone but by the time it was built, it definitely wasn't a small log cabin. We ended up referring to it as HIGH CHAPAREL.

It was wonderful having them so close. Susan was always there to help and was known as our "Crazy aunt" to Claire's kids. She had special ideas on raising kids and what we should all eat to be healthy. Claire and Mike took her suggestions with a grain of salt! Jared after being cared for by Susan while Claire and Mike were away yelled out to his school chums, "Here comes the soup NAZI".

She was so tenderhearted and the local wildlife were always sure of a treat at her house. Our dog, Max, even went down each morning for a treat. We talked her out of going down to our neighbors and asking them why they didn't cover their horses with blankets when it was cold.

In 1995 our lunch group decided to go on a cruise to Alaska. Finally after much planning only two couples were left-Todd and Betty Dooley and Jim and I. The cruise was a great success and we enjoyed the side trip to Butchart Gardens in British Columbia. That trip made me wish we could have spent much longer in Alaska. Later I was able to do just that.

With the Dooleys on cruise to Alaska

MAX

We decided-no, Jim decided he wanted a bird dog so, upon hearing of a family in the Springs that had a German short haired pointer they were trying to find a home for, we went to have a look at him. When we arrived he was chasing butterflies in their small back yard. They said although they loved him, he was too big and energetic for their two small children. We decided to take him for a small fee and as we were leaving they said, "You might want to take his chew log" - LOG??

His name was Chuck. Jim decided that name wasn't proper for a bird dog so he named him Max.

We heard of a dog trainer and so we sent Max to be trained. While at the trainer's house he got loose, barked at a neighbor's chickens and the neighbor shot him with a shot gun. He was hurt badly but recovered. You would think he would be ruined for life at the sound of a gun but not Max. He was always ready to go hunting at the drop of a hat.

He was great with the grandkids although he had some bad habits. He had a voracious appetite and was known to steal any food (like part of a roast beef) from the cabinet if you weren't looking. He thought he was a lap dog and would try to climb on your lap if you showed him any affection. He turned out to be a great bird dog. We finally, after several years, had to put him down. That was a sad day in the Black family.

HOME ON THE RANGE WHERE THE DEER
AND THE ANTELOPE PLAY AND ARE GOOD EATING

The next few years in Woodland Park were uneventful-with usually a deer or elk in the freezer. My birthday was usually during hunting season and I spent many of them tramping through the woods in search of game. Fishing trips made a boat a necessary item. On one occasion Jim and Mike spent hours preparing the boat to camouflage it for duck hunting and came home with 1 duck-we had a duck tasting.

I'm reminded of a piece written by Archibald Rutledge: "Yes, I have brought these boys up to be hunters and I know full well that when the wild creatures need no longer have apprehensions about me, my grandchildren will be hard on their trail pursuing with keen enjoyment and wholesome passion the Sport of Kings while other boys are whirling to the latest jazz tune or telling dubious stories on street corners. I'd like to think that mine are deep in the lonely woods, far in the silent hills listening to another kind of music learning a different kind of lore."

Jim had many hunting and fishing trips with his son-in-law, Mike, and his grandsons. Little Sean when only three came to the house while they were butchering a deer and Claire didn't want him to go out to the garage to see the process I told her, "Let him go-he'll be OK". About 30 minutes later he came back to the house sporting two legs tied around his neck and thrilled to pieces. Sean and Jared today are expert hunters. Jared has taken up bow hunting and came home with a near-trophy antelope. Grandpa had some influence on them.

Sean with trophies

THE GETAWAY CAR

One family crime story that I guess I should confess since the statute of limitations has expired is the "Great Hunting Caper". Many of our hunts were family affairs, usually several family members along on hunting trips. On one occasion several of our family who shall remain nameless (since some are still alive) were driving around an area looking for game. We came upon a large group of deer we passed behind a hill. We got out and hid among the bushes. When the men decided they were close enough they took aim-the deer scattered and Jim took a shot. "I got the big doe", he said as the deer went down. One of us looked through the binoculars & said, "No, it's the buck and he's down". Sure enough it was. What to do now? None of us had a buck tag. The men ran down and pulled the buck into the bushes and we left the scene of the crime.

After the day was over we went back home (about 2 hours away) and Jim was lamenting the fact that he had missed and that all of that deer meat was going to be lost. After much deliberation we decided to go back after it, take our passenger car that had a big trunk and retrieve it. Since it would take 2 men to drag it to the car, a driver was needed to take the car down the road past the area where the deer was hidden, come back and load it in the trunk. The other family members turned "chicken" and said they wanted no part in the caper. So, since the idea to rescue the deer was mine, I was the designated driver. The men took off their hunting clothes, dressed in sport jackets and off we went. We drove to the exact spot. I left them and drove away with instructions to drive down the dark country road several miles and return in 30 minutes. When I got back they had dragged the animal to the side of the road and then proceeded to try to get it in the trunk. Rigor mortis had set in a bit and it was a difficult task, but with a lot of effort it went in the trunk. We then headed for home hoping no policeman would stop us. We drove very carefully and made it back home, hung the deer in the garage and butchered it the next day. My venture into a life of crime ended and I have been law abiding ever since!

Another trip of note was with Susan and Duncan. We went on this trip with the pop-up camper thinking it would be nice to camp out at night and hunt during the day since it was a long drive to and from the hunting area. We hunted all day with no luck and came back to our camper, had a bite to eat and sat around playing cards. A big clap of thunder and bolts of lightning proceeded with pouring rain and whirling wind. The camper was rocking back and forth and it got pretty scary. We finally decided to get out of there. We ran to the car and found the ground so muddy we could hardly walk. The old red hunting car sputtered and groaned and finally pulled us out of the field. We breathed a sigh of relief, drove home and came back several days later to retrieve the camper. That was the last time we took the camper! We had many good times out hunting and it turned into a family sport!

JIM'S WHITE HORSE

Jim had an experience when he was about 18 that somehow lasted his whole life. He was driving home one night when he spotted a white horse lying on the side of the road. He stopped and the horse was still alive so he went to the next town about 2 miles away and reported it to the police. He never knew if the horse was saved but it reappeared many times in his dreams and several times saved him while driving. For many years he nodded off while driving, the white horse appeared and he skidded to a stop. No horse was ever there. Several times when he was riding as a passenger with his son-in-law, Mike, he would drop off to sleep, bolt upright scaring Mike to death, and yell, "Watch out for that white horse in the road!"

There wasn't a horse but Mike was wide awake for many miles while Jim went back to sleep as though nothing happened. The ghost of the white horse was looking after them!

We were busy with our couples' bridge group and lunch bunch. We went to many lunches and plays and made lasting friendships.

We traveled back and forth to Orlando to visit Karen and Barbara and my Dad who was caring for his wife, Ruth. She was suffering from Alzheimer's. He cared for her for over 8 years. Finally on one of our trips I found him exhausted and weakened and talked him into putting her into a nursing home. He visited her twice a day although she had long since forgotten who he was and thought he was her father.

When the problem first started they came to Colorado and we decided on a trip to New Mexico to visit my uncle. We realized she wasn't herself when she wondered why there were so many out of state license plates and was very confused about where we were.

I researched the tour books for the trip and since we were stopping in Santa Fe, I looked for a nice restaurant with local color. I found one with a fountain and Mexican music being played. Dad ordered his dinner and asked for cottage cheese which, of course, they didn't have. After the waiter left he said, "What kind of a place is this, anyway, that they don't have cottage cheese"? OH WELL, I TRIED.

We made our way to Elephant Butte to see our old friends from Venezuela, Bill and Lucille Shivers. They made a big fuss over Dad and even got him on a horse. He always asked about Lucille every time we visited Florida.

Ruth's condition became worse and soon she didn't recognize us when we visited. On one occasion Dad asked her if she knew who we were and I whispered in her ear, "I'm Rita Hayworth" and Jim was Clark Gable. In a moment of clarity she said, "Ha, I didn't think so!"

What a terrible thing Alzheimer's is-much worse for those around you for they are in a world of their own that doesn't exist for anyone else.

After her death, we tried to talk Dad into moving to Colorado, but he loved Florida and said, "It's too cold".

WHERE ARE MY KEYS?

He finally sold his house and moved into a small one and then into a senior apartment that was part of a nursing home where he didn't have to cook anymore. He told me, "I burnt the broccoli and forgot my keys-I'm afraid I'm losing it". I told him I'd done the same, but he was adamant that he should move-he was 95 at the time! At 98 he was still lawn bowling and known as one of their best players! At the senior home he met a very nice lady, Lucille-a retired teacher from Vermont and they became very close "JUST FRIENDS" as they both said. Her family moved her to another place close by and when Dad went to see her the next day-she had died. He was still tooting around in his golf cart during this time.

He was scheduled to come to Colorado for his 100th birthday with Karen and Barbara but had a bad fall so we celebrated his birthday without him. He had a series of falls but never broke a bone-although at 98 he hurt his arm and proceeded to paint the trim on his house with one arm in a sling.

It soon became obvious that he couldn't stay in his apartment by himself anymore so we moved him into the nursing home. Eventually, my 2 daughters brought him to an Orlando nursing home and cared for him for 2 years. I'm so proud of them for taking on that responsibility.

We went to Orlando to celebrate his 103rd birthday and he had pretty much stopped communicating and wasn't enjoying life much although he knew all of the baseball teams-still voted and, with Karen's help, sent birthday cards and $10 to all the grandkids and great grandkids.

While in Alaska I received an email saying he was in the hospital and wasn't expected to live. I made it there on July 2, 2011 and he passed away July 7th with his granddaughter and me by his side-he was 103 1/2.

BACK TO WOODLAND PARK

During this time Karen's son, Ryan, came to spend several summers. Karen, a single mom at this time needed help with him during off school time. So we took him in-not an easy job for "old folks". Jim took him fishing and we took many camping trips. Many of the camping trips were with Ernie and Mollie-one to British Columbia. One to South Dakota to see the Presidents and the beginning of a new monument to Crazy Horse. I think he still remembers these trips with fondness. He is now 35 and has a daughter of his own.

Karen married a fellow employee, Bill McLaughlin, she sold her house and they moved into our old house when Susan and Duncan moved to Colorado. Musical houses!

We arrived in Orlando with plans to take Dad down to the beach for a week at a time share apartment. We got to Orlando and found Jim's sister, Jean, having medical problems.

We had gone on many trips with her and her new husband, George, and thoroughly enjoyed their company. They bought a condo in Colorado Springs. We made a trip to Glacier Park and to Pennsylvania with them. George always researched every town along the way. We depended on him to know all of the history of everyplace we visited. Jim decided once to upstage him by finding out an obscure fact about Wolf Creek Pass that George wouldn't know-how many inches of snow they had per year. As we went over the pass Jim casually mentioned, "They have record snow here" and George knew exactly how many feet and inches to the inch. That was the last time Jim ever tried to upstage George's running commentary as we traveled.

Jean died of cancer on our Orlando trip. She went to the doctor complaining of a back ache. They took a mammogram and found she had breast cancer. After the operation she still had a back ache-and it was worse. It was cancer of the stomach and intestines. She had surgery again and we hurried back to Orlando from the beach. She only lived a few days. It was a shock to all of us. Jean had been a good friend, sister, aunt and mother and we learned a hard lesson, "Check everything out before an operation"!

OUR GRANDIES AND VISITORS

The grandkids were growing up so fast we could hardly believe our eyes. Each one with talents and personalities so different. Sean and Jared were avid hockey players and we went to many hockey games and cheered them on.

Later on we took the pop-up all the way to the Columbia River in British Columbia. Some of the excursions with Ernie and Mollie were our best vacations. We all got along so well and many times spent hours laughing till midnight telling tales of our past experiences in the many foreign countries that we shared together. Seems like they were always there for me and are the 2nd brother and the sister I never had.

We had visits from friends who were curious as to our selection of Colorado as a home and I don't think any of them were disappointed. The Littlefields came and Jim took their 2 little boys on their first fishing excursion. The Coaplands came and we showed off Colorado and we took a trip to New Mexico with them. Sally and Maury came-they both had attended Colorado College and they were excited to return and see some of their old haunts. On our trips to Florida we usually stopped off to see all of them and renew old friendships. Ernie and Mollie decided to return to Colorado and bought a home in La Veta.

Barbara's Nelson came one summer to attend the Cripple Creek Film Festival. The film that he helped produce won the top award. It was called 'The First of May'. It's still available in Colorado but somehow never made it to the big time even though it starred Julie Harris, Mickey Rooney and had a cameo with Joe DiMaggio.

WHERE NOW

John finished junior college in Kilgore and came back home to Colorado to finish at The Univ of Co in Colorado Springs.

John finally decided to leave home. He fell in love with Cathy a beautiful blond who lived in Colorado Springs. She had been divorced twice and had 3 children-not the credentials for a new daughter-in-law, but after meeting her we decided he had made a good choice. Her oldest was Dustin about to be a teenager. JC and Britney were 5 and 7. Their western wedding was held in Claire's living room. Claire's 2 girls and Britney were dressed in cowboy boots and hats with flowers attached. JC gave the bride away. Cathy made it all the way to the altar without remembering her flowers. The minister directed a rescue of the bouquet and the deed was done. Cathy became known to my girls as the "favorite daughter". Our old friends Ernie and Mollie were there and John's best friend from Kilgore and Indonesia days made it in from Tulsa.

All seemed to be going just the way we hoped retirement would be. Jim was hunting and fishing and having a great time- I was busy with bridge, church and social club affairs. We were nearing our 50th year of marriage.

THE S—HIT THE FAN

Jim started having kidney problems. We went to our local Doctor and he finally referred us to urology specialists. They said the kidney must be removed. My brother and his wife were adamant that we should come to Pittsburgh to see a specialist who they considered to be the best in the country. We travelled there in December, 1999. After a battery of tests, Dr Cohen did the operation. At first they said it was a success and then the dreaded word, CANCER. We came home to find the Christmas tree up and the house decorated with lights. The next course was radiation treatment and chemo.

By July things were going well. The kids had planned a big celebration for our 50th anniversary so we scheduled an appointment for MD Anderson the next week.

The party was a huge success. All of the family participated in a lively song and dance, "I'm Going to Love You Forever" in cowboy boots and hats. The grandkids did a show on their own –all directed by Claire, our drama major. Many local friends attended as well as many who travelled from afar. Bill McLaughlin was master of ceremonies and asked everyone to get up and tell where they met us. Both Jim and I had a great time and lots of laughs.

Our old friends, Maury and Sally, couldn't come. Sally was under treatment for lung cancer. She and Jim commiserated by phone on their different treatments and medications. Life was never the same for us the next year.

We embarked on our usual trip to Florida the 1st of May and stopped in Houston to see Earl and Ruth Goin who were in declining health and then on to see Sally who was in very serious condition and barely knew us. My parting words to her were, "We'll get together some day and prepare some midnight chicken" (referring to a family joke about barbequing chicken that took much longer than expected and we had to wait long into the night for it to be cooked).

We went on to Florida and were there about a week when Maury called and said Sally was gone.

Jim had a bad turn about that time so we had to cut our vacation short and hurry back to Colorado. The girls all took turns in helping care for him. Mike came almost every day at noon to take Jim for a short ride-Mike was like a son to Jim-they were hunting and fishing buddies and spent many hours together.

Finally, the battle was over on September 17, 2001, just 6 days after the 9/11 bombing. He never knew about that tragedy.

I'll never forget the kindness of our many friends and the help of our children during those bleak days. The funeral was held on September 24th. The church was filled and we had letters and cards from people I never expected to hear from.

My life seemed to end too. On the night of Jim's death the girls were all in the living room talking and telling funny stories of their childhood laughing hysterically. Jim was asleep in his chair. I, exhausted, had gone to bed. I heard them in my semi-sleep stage and smiled to myself. This laughter was the last sounds Jim heard on earth. The laughter of his children. What could be a better sound? Claire came in several hours later and said, "Mom, I think he's gone". His wedding ring had slipped off his finger and was on the floor beside him.

Jim and partner on one of his last hunts in England

OUR FATHER

In1950, you married our mother, Grace
And whisked her away to Venezuela, oh what a place!
You worked drilling for oil, that bubbling crude,
and made a great life for you and your brood.

There were five of us kids, you brought us so much joy,
Karen, Susan, Barbara, Claire and John, the only boy.
You had many good friends we are happy to recall,
And showed us the importance of kindness to all.

You were strength and security, laughter and fun,
A prince to your daughters, a pal to your son.
You guided us with love and took time to teach,
Each of us our potential and the goals we could reach.

Because of your work we were fortunate to live,
In most parts of the world, what a great gift to give!
You fulfilled Mom's dreams of travel to exotic places
You led the way, counting kids and suitcases.

Then you retired to Colorado, where the sky is so blue,
Where hunting and fishing were dreams come true.

We are blessed with the years that we had together,
There are so many memories of you that we'll always treasure.

A father whose heart we knew we could trust,
A father who brought out the best in us.
A father who knew and cared enough to say
The encouraging words that paved the way.

You were sentimental and precious to the end
We know in our hearts we will see you again.
Your courage travels with you, your example is left behind,
So that we will all remember the sweetness of your time.

You made our lives richer and the world a better place,
DAD, WE LOVE YOU AND WE WILL MISS YOUR SMILING FACE!

This poem was written by all of his girls and Claire read it at the funeral.

Many of our friends from Venezuela days came to the service and Maury Hammond came from Houston-he and Jim were the best of friends for years and I had a soft spot in my heart for him. It turned out to be love.

ALONE

The next several years were a blur to me. What would possibly become of me after 51 years of marriage? The kids were so helpful. Duncan came up and installed a bolt on my kitchen door. I had never been afraid before.

I went to Branson with Claire Mike and grandkids for Thanksgiving and we all nearly lost it when Andy Williams sang, "It will be a Blue Christmas Without You". Gradually I began to feel like myself again and came to the realization that I would be an OLD WIDOW for the rest of my life.

THE BIG FIRE

That next year was the year of the Hayman fire. Woodland Park was surrounded by smoke and the fire came closer each day. I finally decided to pack up all of my valuables and leave town if necessary. When I could see the fire over the trees, I took my prized possessions and went to Colorado Springs and moved in with my friends, Nancy and Chuck McKesson. They opened their home to me and my "stuff" and I stayed there 2 weeks. Susan and Duncan held the fort, packed up and were ready to leave on a moment's notice. Fortunately, the wind changed when the fire was 7 miles away and we were spared. It was heartwarming to have such good friends.

Wildflower new growth after the Hayman fire

I did realize, however, that possessions aren't that important and if this ever happened again, I'd only take my jewelry, photos, important papers and, maybe, my fur coat!

ONE BABY STEP

New Years Eve 2003 we were sitting around the table and discussing our New Year's resolutions. I was the last after all of the family promised, "I'll do this and I want to do that-OK, Mom, what about you?" I said, "I'm going out and meet some new friends."

My first baby step was to go to Florida. My good friends, Ernie and Mollie invited me to stop off in Houston. Another good friend called about that time and said she had just been to Maury Hammond's 70th birthday party and gave me all the latest news about Maury and his family. After talking to her I picked up the phone-called Maury and asked, "Why wasn't I invited?" I said, "I'm coming to Houston soon and I want to go dancing". He was a little taken aback but he courageously said "Just let me know when you're coming." Several weeks later, Mollie called and said, "Well, when are you coming? Maury has been calling to see if you are here yet."

Little did I know that this phone call would change my life forever-yes, we did go dancing and Ernie and Mollie came along as chaperones-imagine 2 70 year-olds needing a chaperone!

My next trip to Houston was to attend the 50th wedding anniversary of my dear friends, Nancy and Chuck Mckesson. Chuck was undergoing cancer treatment and was in very poor health so I really wanted to be there to help in the celebration. I called my friend, Maury, to see if he would drive me over to Austin. We had a great time and Maury proved to be a very considerate escort even though he didn't know the McKessons that well. He stayed with his daughter and I stayed with Nancy and Chuck. This would be the last time I would ever see Chuck again.

FRIENDSHIP CRUISE

Take me sailing

Shortly after the party, Maury called and invited me on a Caribbean Cruise organized by an old friend from Nigeria, Patsy Craton. (I think she put him up to the call). Just before boarding the ship, I got word of Chuck's death. The cruise was wonderful and I made a lot of new friends from the Houston area. As soon as the cruise was over, I went to Austin to stay with Nancy for awhile and Maury went on a trip to Big Bend with his Boston lady friend. Not much going on here in the way of romance-just good friends who had a lot of common background and mutual friends.

Later Maury made a trip to Colorado in July and we really enjoyed each other's company. We had dinner with some friends and they told me, "We think he's a keeper" Up till that time I hadn't considered keeping anyone! After July 4 we went to Creede and Lake City.

VIVA MEXICO

In August we took a trip to San Miguel de Allende with some friends who we met at Nancy and Chuck's party. We traveled there by bus and stayed there a week. It was great fun and it seemed we were made for each other. On our return we talked about what the future would hold for us and decided that the future would certainly be perfect if we spent it together!

We announced our intentions at a Christmas party in the home of our Houston friends on December 8th and I went back to Colorado to face the music (my kids). They all liked Maury but weren't sure of his intentions! HA, seemed like I used those words several times in the past on them! Now the tables were turned!

WEDDING BELLS

Maury was to come for Christmas and I told him to bring his suit. We met with my minister and she said she could do the ceremony the day after Christmas. We tried to get the Catholic priest to take the part but that didn't work out.

I called Ernie and Mollie and asked them what they were doing for Christmas and they said they would be in Denver for Christmas with their daughter and were returning home the day after Christmas. I said, "How would you like to be in a wedding?" The answer was, "We'll be there, is my green dress OK?" The wedding was on!

Newlyweds with chaperones, Ernie and Mollie Haynes

FAST FORWARD

Susan and Claire were a big help. Paula did the flowers. All the grandkids were home for Christmas so they could attend. I wore my red Christmas dress. Our minister announced that there was going to be a surprise wedding after church and all were welcome to stay! John walked me down the aisle and when the preacher asked who gives this woman, the whole family stood up and said, "We do."

We had a small reception at a local restaurant and my brother and his Denver family were there. We embarked on our new life together not only with family approval but what we felt would be the approval of Sally and Jim!

2nd I DO

Shortly after New Years we traveled back to Houston and made arrangements to be married at Maury's church January 10th. We invited our Houston friends and Maury's family. His son and daughter-in-law stood up with us and their daughter, Sarah, was the flower girl. It was a very nice ceremony and made Maury feel like the Catholic Church approved the union. We had a nice luncheon after the ceremony so were soundly married, not only once, but twice!

STARTING OVER – GET THE DUMPSTER

The next month or so was very trying, getting Maury's house ready for sale, trying to get 17 year's accumulation dispersed among his family and getting rid of the rest; a 30 foot dumpster load! We packed up the things Maury wanted to keep and ended up with an accumulation of boxes which still take up the major part of my garage in Woodland Park 9 years later!

GOODBYE FRED

Our next major hurdle was finding a home for Fred, Maury's African Grey parrot. Fred took a dislike to me on our first encounter. He had a history of dislike for women and had bitten almost all of the female relatives. We fixed his cage with plexiglas around the bottom so small girls couldn't get their fingers inside. Maury Jr was thrilled to get Fred. That lasted about 1 month. We got a call, "Dad, you need to find another home for Fred. He bit Karen and we just can't keep him." Maury called Andrew, his son-in-law in Pennsylvania who loved Fred and he showed up the next day to load up Fred and furniture Terry wanted. Fred ruled the roost in Foglesville as he and Andrew were birds of a feather. We visited him a year later and he bit Maury! Fred finally made it to bird heaven in 2013 at the age of 35.

OFF WE GO

We finally sold the house and packed up Maury's things. He's still accusing me of throwing away things he can't find. I told his family they owe me a huge debt as I saved them from having to do that cleanup job.

We headed out for Woodland Park in a U-Haul truck towing Maury's Ford Explorer. It was an experience of a lifetime and we decided that since we made it through without a divorce, we could make it through anything!

Maury and Sally had attended Colorado College years ago and Maury felt like he was coming home albeit a new home but at least a place he was familiar with. He delivered chicken dinners during school in the '50s and still thinks he knows his way around the Springs- WRONG.

We joined the Lake George Gem and Mineral Club and Maury was accepted without reservation by my Colorado friends and family. We were ready to face the world of two old folks starting life anew. It was to be a bigger challenge than we expected.

We attended the Catholic and Protestant churches every Sunday and were feeling that we had all the bases covered. We were travelling to Texas to see Maury's family and to Florida to tend to my Dad who was becoming unable to live alone due to various falls.

And yes, we still went dancing and continue to this day. One big laugh was at the Broken Spoke in Austin when a lady crossed the floor and asked if we were married. We said, "Yes, we're newlyweds." Her reply was, "Our table was discussing you and decided you must not be old married folks-you were having too much fun.

We've been complimented many times at dance halls and the most recent time was at the Chicken, Alaska, 4th of July party on the gravel parking lot where a lady took our picture and when she showed it to us said, "I'm taking this home to my kids to show them that old folks can still have fun". I guess that was a compliment!

About this time wsse got word from Karen that she and Bill were getting divorced. I was sorry to see this happen but Bill in his quest for success in the business world lost his moral footing and forgot that Karen had played a big part in his success.

He did become a father for Ryan and gave Ryan his name which was no small thing. Ryan is now becoming reacquainted with his own father and he has a little girl, Jada, of his own. He is a wonderful father giving her all the attention he missed himself.

One trip we made about this time was to Riverside, Connecticut, to see Lucy, Maury's sister, and his granddaughter, Audrey, who has a job in NYC. We went to Audrey's apartment in Brooklyn and wondered why anyone would choose to live there. We also attended Maury's aunt Edwina's 99th birthday. We rented a car and drove to Cape Cod. I found an ad in the newspaper that sounded good and off we went. We arrived in Hyannis Port and found our hotel-it was called Cuddles and Bubbles-not in the ad. The big plus to the place was a huge bathtub for 2 bottles of bubbles and 2 huge white towels! Much more exciting was the tour to see the whales! We bought 2 coffee cups with the hotel's name on them to remind us that we had been there and done that!

The next summer we went to Lucy's to help celebrate Edwina's 100th and flew down to Pittsburgh to see my brother and sister-in-law who was battling cancer. She met us at the airport but we soon realized she wasn't herself and I had the feeling that would be the last time we would ever see her. She was a nurse practitioner and spent her life in service to the sick and now it hardly seemed right that she found herself unable to help herself. She was a great lady and one of my heroes. In December, we got word that she was losing her battle and the next time we were in Pittsburgh was to attend her funeral, 4 months later.

Susan was ailing. She had breast cancer and had been trying all manner of holistic remedies, much of which I was unaware. She finally decided to go to Mexico to a clinic she had researched and felt had the treatment for her. Karen, Barb, Duncan, Maury and I took turns staying with her during her 8 week treatment. When she returned and at the clinic's recommendation, she went to an oncologist in the Springs who was open to Susan's ideas of holistic medicine. In a short time, however, and at the insistence of family she started chemo with high hopes of recovery.

We were all hopeful and for awhile she seemed to be improving. Maury and I took her to most of her appointments, Maury patiently waiting with me for hours during treatments and appointments. He was my anchor to lean on during this time. Finally we all realized she wasn't going to get better. What can you do when you see your precious child dying before your very eyes? We all got through this time leaning on each other. Karen and Barb coming from Florida to help and care for her. Duncan with a great measure of patience and love helping her through her last days. She found great comfort in her church and friends there and other friends they had made. All who knew her in her quest to help others, for she had been doing elder care for 8 years, knew her as a happy, joyful, laughing person and a light went out for all of us when she died in my and Duncan's arms.

Her funeral was attended by many people in the community who knew and loved her. Her sister, Claire gave the eulogy.

After the service during which it poured rain and lightning and thunder, we left the church and a beautiful rainbow covered Woodland Park. Her burial was next to her dad in our back yard. The family all there, Maury playing the guitar, Claire Barbara and Maury singing at my request, "I'll Fly Away".

The end of a beautiful life and an arrow in the hearts of all of us. Until the day we meet again! And now I was thankful the good lord sent me Maury who held me up and comforted me during one of the most trying times of my life.

GOLD

Sometime during our second year Maury got reunited with an old college friend, Ron Timroth, with whom he had gone to Alaska prospecting for gold in 1958. That experience didn't turn out too well but Maury always wondered what became of him. They found gold, staked claims, and Maury signed over his interest in the claims to Ron for an air ticket home. I encouraged Maury to try to find him. He found on the Internet that Ron had been the president of a model airplane club in the Springs which led to his finding Ron in Snowmass. They made arrangements for a visit. They had a wonderful time and his wife, Zana, was just as happy for them as I. We became fast friends and that greatly affected our future.

Ron and Maury decided they would like to revisit their old prospecting days and go back to Alaska where they had been 50 years ago. Susan was pretty sick at the time and Maury was reluctant to leave. They settled on early September, 2008, for a 2 week trip. It was the trip of a lifetime for Maury and he and Ron were both anxious to revisit their youth. They both caught "Gold fever". They got back in mid September and Susan seemed to be awaiting Maury's return. She met Ron and after he left to go back to Snowmass, she lived 6 more days.

From that moment on our lives were filled with phone calls, Internet searches, plots and sub plots on how to get back to Alaska and find the gold that was waiting for these 2 clever fellows to find. After months of planning it was decided they would go in June, 2009. I, not wanting to be left behind, decided, like it or not, I would go too! After all wasn't my whole life so far a life of a CAMP FOLLOWER? What difference could a gold camp be to an oil camp?

We were busy making arrangements for Alaska in June via the Princess Line from Vancouver. In preparation we, gathered up all our camping gear and sent it ahead with some old clothes and I prepared to be the only woman along with 8 other miners!

OFF TO ALASKA

Shortly before leaving, I came down with a pain on my left side. It was pretty bad so I thought I'd better get the Doctor to confirm my diagnosis that it was diverticulitis. My regular Doctor was booked so I decided I would go to our new hospital and saw a new young Doctor who had a practice there. He thought it would be a good idea to do a cat scan since I was getting ready to go to Alaska and be away for several months so I did the scan. He called the next day said sure enough it was diverticulitis but the scan also showed a tumor on my right kidney that was probably cancer. The next week or so I saw an oncologist and a surgeon and it was recommended that I see a urologist. Well, our trip was scheduled for June 7th and, when I called my brother, he suggested I come to Pittsburgh to see the same Doctor that treated Jim 8 years ago. I made an appointment to see Dr Cohen in 4 weeks and we sailed off to Alaska as planned.

College Fjord and Harvard Glacier

Team Alaska

Team Alaska plus boss

Entrance to Uhler Creek Mine

View of Uhler Creek from our camper

Moose dining room in Chicken, Ak

Ours is the spacious pop-up on the right

We stayed in Chicken for 2 weeks after arriving in Anchorage in 7 days. Maury went each day down to the claim on Uhler Creek and I went several times with him but mostly stayed in Chicken. I can't say it was the best of vacations with a possible operation for cancer hanging over my head, but I tried to be positive and hopeful. We left Chicken after 2 weeks and made our way via Fairbanks to Pittsburgh arriving late on July 6 with an appointment at 10:00 AM July 7.

OPERATION POSSIBLE

Dr Cohen ordered many more tests, sent for the scan done in Colorado, and suggested I get my gall bladder removed too. By the time all of the tests were taken I scheduled an appointment with another doctor for the gall bladder. He had a week's vacation planned and the verdict was that the kidney would be removed-it was cancer in a place where the tumor itself couldn't be removed. So I was scheduled for surgery on August 9th, the day after Dr Young came back from vacation.

We took a short trip to Orlando to see Dad and help Karen move from her house in Bay Hill.

We stayed with my brother and had the use of his old car (he just bought a new one) so we drove across Pennsylvania to see Maury's daughter, Terry (where Fred, the parrot, lived), in Eastern PA and went on to Connecticut to see his sister, Lucy and his granddaughter, Audrey.

We drove back in time to take all of the preps on Friday for the surgery the following Monday. I checked into the hospital; not what you would call a great vacation and definitely not recommended. I'd have preferred "Cuddles and Bubbles".

All went well. I was in the hospital for 5 days, came home to my brother's with the words of the Doctor, "All borders benign-you are cured!" My prayers were answered-not completely as I was hoping I wouldn't lose the kidney but I was cancer free and needed no further treatment. I owe my life to that young doctor in Woodland Park for I never would have caught the tumor so early!

We had the opportunity and time to get reacquainted with my old school chum and bridesmaid, Peggy Dolan and her husband. We spent several lunch and dinner dates remembering the good old days and catching up on our lives.

We headed back to Colorado driving Bob's car to deliver it to his son in Denver. I made the trip easily and Maury was very considerate going over the bumps with great care.

We stopped off in St Louis to visit Susan and Joe Mckee. It had been a long time since I had seen them. Joe was now in assisted living and the three of us went there and had lunch with him. It was the first time they had met Maury and we left with their stamp of approval!

It was good to be home! I thought my health problems were over but this didn't prove to be true. Seems like old age gets a hold of you no matter what and I guess I was finally reaching that time in life.

HEART BEAT

One of the tests I took in Pittsburgh was with a cardiologist. She changed my blood pressure medicines and said I should see a cardiologist in 6 months not telling me much more than she thought the new meds would solve the problem-PROBLEM-WHAT PROBLEM?

I didn't think to ask. I finally got around to making an appointment in the Springs and the Doctor said after looking at the Pittsburgh tests, "I guess you know you're in heart failure!!"

Hence a battery of new tests and a recommendation for a defibrillator-pacemaker that should keep me alive awhile longer! I was in a mild state of shock but had to make the decision to have the darn thing put in before summer as we were planning to go to Alaska again to continue Maury's quest for gold!

All went according to schedule although I awoke during surgery and asked why I was hurting so much and they discovered my IV with the anesthesia had come out. What next? The good lord must throw a curve every now and then to make sure you're listening.

We went to Florida to celebrate my Dad's 102nd birthday. We took him first to Karen's for cake, ice cream and presents then to Al Capone's, a dinner floor show. The girls said it would be a waste of time as he would sleep through the whole thing. The show went on and he never closed his eyes. They put a spotlight on him and wished him a happy birthday. He was proud as punch!

The next day we all went out to eat at a popular restaurant near Karen's new home. After a second martini Maury tried to get up and couldn't-he was unable to speak clearly-we left in a hurry, took him home, got him in the house where he fell while trying to get up from the couch and still having trouble talking. Karen called 911-it was a mini stroke and he spent 2 days in the hospital.

We had driven to Houston, left our car there and flew on to Florida. We missed our flight to Houston and had to wait 4 days to get out because of Spring Break traffic. We finally arrived in Houston-me sick with another diverticulitis attack-Maury doing OK. Maury went out to eat with Maury Jr and family for "crawdads" and came back with food poisoning. Our poor friends, the Littlefields had 2 sickies to care for and Isabel nursed us back to health with special Portuguese soups and sent us on our way "much the worse for wear". I got back in time for my new "heartbeat helper" operation and Maury was fit as a fiddle.

We spent the next week or two looking for a camper to take to Alaska with the idea of parking it at the claim. Four weeks went by-I was doing OK so we left in Maury's new pickup towing a 35 foot camper and drove to Alaska. It took 9 days. We camped along the way. When we arrived at Mile Post 103 on the Taylor Hwy, the turn off to the claims on Uhler Creek, one of the men looked at our camper and said he couldn't see how we were going to get it down to the site. It started to rain and the roads became almost impassable. We camped at MP 103 for several days waiting on weather. We could get to the claim in the pickup and Maury mentioned to Ron we were thinking of moving down the highway to a campground on Walker Fork about 30 minutes from 103. The next AM the whole crew arrived and said, "We're taking you down today!" They loaded the camper on a flatbed trailer, tied it down, hitched the trailer to a 5 ton dump truck and we followed in the pickup. That night they stopped about a mile from the claim on a steep hill and said, "Tomorrow we'll bring the dozer and pull you in". We had to use a ladder to get in the camper. The inside was in pretty good shape. We slept in the bed on a steep slant. Bright and early they all came back and took us the rest of the way. There were 8 serious switchbacks and somehow, with the expertise of one Glenn Mehan, we arrived at the gold claim with only a few scratches on one rear corner of the camper. However, it was there to stay; getting it out was impossible without cutting it up into small pieces.

We had email via a satellite dish but no other means of communication as voice (Skype) was spotty at best. We were settled in now; a lovely location with a bubbling creek alongside the camper. Everything was operational and except for terrible weather, we were there for the duration of the mining season, which for us would be September 1st. The weather was most unusual; rain, rain, rain. The main road to Chicken was closed twice because of flooding; one week each time and we were getting short of fuel and drinking water which we had been hauling from Chicken. We used creek water for dishes and bathing and it was rather muddy from the rains. The little bubbling brook turned several times into a rushing torrent and we worried it would sweep us away. We had evacuation plans in mind but, fortunately, we didn't have to use them.

Our trip to Alaska this time was filled with incredible scenery. We went to Fairbanks several times for machine parts. The last time barely making it back on semi flooded roads. Tok is the closest real town-not much there-a grocery store (has the best apple fritters outside of Houston), laundromat, some shops, motels, cell phone communication. It's about a 4 hour drive from camp. One hour, 7 ½ miles, on a terrible road with several mud holes that are hardly passable to the Taylor Hwy, 1 hr to Chicken and 1 1/2 to 2 hrs to Tok.

One of my favorite shops in Alaska is Bonny Achman's place, Jack Wade Gold, in Tok. She showed us a nugget her husband found that weighs 56 ¾ troy ounces. At $1400/toz and 900 fine (90% pure gold) it's worth $72,000 as bullion. She's been offered $200,000 for it but it's still hers. Value goes up for collector and jewelry grade gold. The nugget is called 'The Prospector'. With a little imagination you can see the back of a partially bald, bearded man with his right arm circling a pan. Maury got a picture taken of it in his hand.

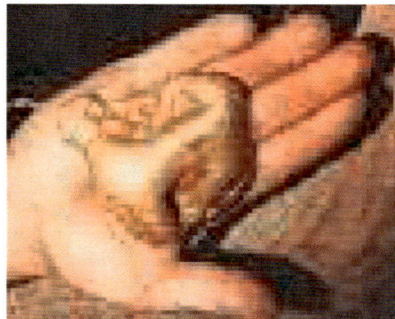

Jack Wade Gold, Tok, AK

A lot of time was spent setting up new machinery (wash plant). Several sites were tested for gold with very sketchy results. One site, however, 3 miles upstream from camp yielded 1 ounce of gold per yard of gravel BONANZA! It will have to wait for BLM approval and maybe a road built for access-1, 2, maybe 3years? Total gold recovery for the summer was less than 30 ounces.

Maury, Glenn, Ron, Jerry & Grant; miners at Uhler Creek, AK

What does a camp follower do? I started writing my life story, did pastels, read a lot and learned a lot about looking for gold. The satisfaction on the faces of the men when they find a nugget is unbelievable-they are like little boys with their first bike, baseball mitt or Red Ryder BB gun.

We left Uhler at the end of August and had an easy time (no heavy camper!) getting back to Woodland Park in 6 days.

GARDEN OF EDEN

On our third trip to Alaska we stopped at Eden, UT, to attend Sean and Whitney's wedding. Eden is just east of Ogden in the mountains. Both Sean and Whitney graduated from the Air Force Academy in May. We were at the graduation and it was very impressive-the Blue Angels put on a flying exhibition. Sean looked so handsome in his uniform. His grandfather looking down on this occasion must have been very proud of him and all of the hard work he had to endure to have this day of celebration. Needless to say I was pretty proud too!

The wedding was so beautiful held in the backyard of Whitney's parents' house. Huge yellow wildflowers in bloom and it truly looked like the 'Garden of Eden'. Jessie and Cara were bridesmaids-all grown up now and looking beautiful in their yellow dresses carrying big orange and red daisies.

Jared, Cara, Jessie, Sean, Whitney, Claire, Mike

Karen called while we were at the wedding saying Dad was in the hospital but he was doing OK and rolling his eyes when they suggested he take some new medicine. So we decided to continue on.

Since our big RV had been left at the gold camp and would likely stay there, we had decided to buy a pop-up camper, camp along the way then park it at MP 103 or in Tok. Maury had trouble keeping batteries charged last summer so he got a solar system to try out.

The trip up was mostly uneventful except for a flat on the pop-up. We found the spare tire flat too and were contemplating leaving the pop-up and driving to the nearest road house when a couple stopped and offered their portable air compressor. We got the spare inflated and limped into Whitehorse where we got 2 new tires. We made it the rest of the way and parked the pop-up in Tok.

We got an email from Karen saying Dad was failing. We went to Tok to use the cell phone. Had trouble getting reservations to fly to Florida. Spike Jorgenson, owner of a gift store, took us to his house, got on his computer and got me reservations. We went to Fairbanks where I caught a plane south. I arrived on July 1st and he lived until July 7th. The weather was nice until that day-dark clouds, rain and lightening all day and he passed peacefully on to his reward. He had round-the-clock hospice care. I was now left without my dear father but was thankful that I had him so many years with so many good memories.

I made my way back to Fairbanks where Maury met me.

We took a short trip to Denali Park. Mt McKinley was socked in which is not uncommon. We stayed overnight just outside the park and visited a sled dog kennel owned by a winner of the Iditarod and Yukon Quest races, Jeff King, who put on quite a show for a bunch of tourists. Very interesting. Then, on to Valdez where we went salmon fishing and caught 5 apiece (I caught the big one). We had them frozen and sent them to Duncan to keep for us. We took some salmon to Whitney's parents who have a home near Wasilla. Mrs Palin was out of town so we didn't get a chance to visit!

Things weren't going well at the claim. Ron and Glenn were at odds and we were on Glenn's side. Maury and Ron had a talk and Ron told Maury, "You're free to go". We headed to Fairbanks to sell Maury's guns. We got to Chicken and Maury sold the guns to Bronk Jorgenson who mines gold, and runs a large trailer park. We returned to the claim and sold the camper and solar system to Ron. So, after confronting floods, bears, impossible roads, etc, etc, etc, Maury finally gave up due to differences over the mining operation. It was a good experience in all but unfortunate it had to end. So, we left our RV home in the wilds of Alaska.

ALASKANS WHO HELPED US

Mike, Lou and Josea Busby
Mike and Lou run Chicken Gold Camp in Chicken, an RV Park, gift shop and snack bar. Mike restored the gold dredge, Pedro, and moved it onto his property. He also mines gold nearby and lets people pan his dirt for a fee. Josea, Mike and Lou's daughter, installed a satellite dish and modem for an Internet connection on Uhler Creek.

Sue Wren
Sue works very hard running a restaurant, bar, package store, gift shop and sells gas in Chicken. She threatened her mother with a butcher knife for smoking inside the restaurant one time in front of us. She turned out to be a good friend.

Dick and Robin Hammond
Robin is postmistress in Chicken. Dick mines gold, traps fur bearing animals, is President of Forty Mile Miners Assoc and is a ham radio operator. Maury buys pay dirt from Dick and pans out the gold. Not an economical way to collect gold but by far the cheapest so far!

Bronk, Thor, Pearl and Spike Jorgenson
Bronk and his brother, Thor, run an RV park, gift shop, rent cabins, sell gas, diesel and propane in Chicken and mine gold. They are thinking of establishing a mining museum and have looked at several of Ron's dozers, etc., on Uhler Creek. Pearl, Bronk and Thor's mother, in Tok runs one of the best gift shops in AK. Her encased moose outside is very impressive. Spike has a world class collection of trophy game mounts in his house and was instrumental in getting me plane reservations to get to FL in time to see my Dad before he passed.

Bruce Hammond

Bruce worked in the Chemistry Dept of the U of AK at Fairbanks. He knew Louie Schene, previous owner of the Uhler Creek claims, and helped Louie mine during the summer. We visited him and his wife in Fairbanks who took quite a while cleaning off spaces for us to sit down. Her house was that cluttered-which didn't bother Maury at all!

On the way back to Woodland Park we stopped off to see the Buzardes in Dutch John, Utah, where Buz and Renee have a beautiful home high on the mountain. Buz was recovering from an adverse reaction to new heart medicine several weeks previous to our arrival and he and Maury decided it was time to test his resistance to alcohol. After several stiff drinks it was apparent that alcohol was stimulating each of them. The next morning Buz was extremely cheerful and when he saw us off both he and Maury decided he had fully recovered from medical problems.

OFF TO GEORGIA

The summer before going to Georgia in 2012 we had a busy schedule; two big graduations to attend. First was my granddaughter, Aislinn's, from Rollins College in Orlando. She was honored with a Fulbright Scholarship and her accomplishments were recounted in the commencement speech. Her next step will be Malaysia.

We then travelled to South Bend for Maury's grandson, Trey's graduation from Notre Dame. He was an honor student in Chemical Engineering. What a beautiful campus. We stayed in a student dorm for 2 nights and most of Maury's family were there.

We were invited to dinner by one of Trey's roommate's parents and, believe it or not, there was a man there who was from a town very close to Alvear, Argentina, where I had lived during Jim's assignment in Argentina. Small world!

We were off to Georgia in our new 35 foot camper in quest for gold. Maury got a new toy, Gold Hog, to use while mining. We spent one week there at a pay-to-mine place on a 'river' (small stream) and the most gold we found was in the packaged dirt they sold at the company store! Maury spent 3 days with a man we met camped next to us who was dredging on a club claim downstream and he was a guest. Maury found a few colors. Barbara joined us there, did some panning for gold and gems (in packaged dirt), and we went on to Austin, Texas, to attend the Anaco reunion where Barbara had a ball visiting with schoolmates from Escuela Anaco.

OFF THROUGH THE CORNFIELDS

We traveled one summer up to Claire and Mike's cabin in Wisconsin. We took JC, John's son, with us and we were all amazed at the miles after miles of cornfields. JC said he slept several hours and woke up seeing the same cornfield. We arrived safely and had a wonderful vacation. Claire and I scoured the small town shops and the boys showed Maury where the big fish were biting in the lake. Claire's dog, Tasha, stood with Maury on the dock for hours never tiring although she was getting quite old. They made quite a pair; she getting more excited than Maury whenever he got a fish hooked. Jessie, Cara and the boys were getting to be experts in water sports and fishing.

On our way home we decided that we had had enough driving and pulled into a small town, Chanute, Kansas. To my surprise the welcome sign for the city said, "The home of Osa Johnson-see the museum". The museum didn't open till 10:00 AM but I told Maury we would just have to wait and spend another night. What were the chances that I would meet up with Osa again after all of these years? I thought somehow we were soul mates. The museum was a beautiful tribute to a very clever lady who became an author, hunter, and movie star. Look her up on Google-she would be an inspiration to any young person and still is mine.

LIFE WITH MAURY

Maury has 4 children and 8 grandchildren. I have 4 children, 8 grandchildren and 1 great grandchild so we've doubled our blessings.

Since we both had long marriages it took awhile to adjust to our new one. One thing we did learn was don't expect the SAME!

Maury, with some help from me, decided to retire when I found out he was due on a drilling rig in West Texas 2 weeks after we were married! We would have lots of time to see the rest of the world. Little did I know that meant "off to Alaska", digging for aquamarines on Mt Antero, a fourteener, roaming the mountains of Colorado and looking for precious stones!

Most of Maury's family have come for visits to Woodland Park and I think have all decided that he is in good hands and has found a great place to spend his retirement years

Debbie and family spent a week's vacation and enjoyed skiing with Dad.

Terry and Andrew came for a week and did a whirlwind tour of the area, made it to the top of Pikes Peak and we all had a great time.

One rather dubious visit was Maury Junior and family who came during the Christmas holiday. We had great plans for them-a week in Breckenridge at my time share. That week turned into what you might call "The vacation from hell". Upon arriving in Breckenridge, we found they had mistakenly rented our place and we were eventually assigned to another at 11,000 feet altitude-a little high for flatlanders. The first day M Jr's car had problems and when Maury tried to pull him out of the parking lot, he slid back into Jr's car and damaged both cars. Their oldest daughter, Sarah, was signed up for ski school and flat out refused to go. Let's go ice skating! Maury & M Jr had to show off their ice skating skills and Maury ended up at the emergency room with a bad cut on his nose. Then Rebecca got altitude sickness so we all decided to go back to Woodland Park and take her to the emergency room. On Christmas Eve we all went to church and prayed for guidance. They left town I'm sure vowing never to return. They did several times with much better results!

Audrey, Maury's granddaughter, came for a long weekend and we all enjoyed her visit.

Lucy, Maury's sister, came twice and was a wonderful guest and great to be around. She is truly a gem. All-in-all I think we passed the test as happily married old folks.

I encouraged Maury to go to the 50th reunion for the Colorado College class of 1955 which was a bust. He took a five year course and also graduated with the Class of 1956 so he attended that reunion, saw a lot of his old football team mates and had a great time.

Maury had a successful career in the oil business travelling to many countries (13); Libya, Ireland, Nigeria, Syria, Sudan, Tunisia, Germany, Canada, Indonesia, Pakistan, Kuwait, Egypt and Kazakhstan. So he's covered a lot of places in the past. The time in Kuwait was working with firefighters putting out the fires started by Saddam Hussein. The only good thing to come out of Saddam's reign of terror was blue glass formed by the intense heat of the fires fusing the sand around some of the well heads. Maury brought some home and gave me a piece which I had made into a beautiful pendant.

He was raised on a cattle ranch near Cody, Wyoming, and almost became a cowboy/dude wrangler/hunting guide. While he was in high school he worked 2 summers for a dude ranch including two 3-week pack trips over the continental divide to Jackson Hole. They also took out hunters on horseback to hunting camps in the fall-he thought he could work up to "guide". He's been to many places I've never been, so between us we've pretty much been everywhere except China and Russia. Where can we go next? California?

We made several trips to Cody to visit the "old ranch" that was owned by his maternal grandfather. The first time we went there the lady who had been the ranch manager's wife was still living, Audrey Wilde, and she filled out a lot of his old memories of the ranch. The second time we visited Ester Johansen, the daughter of the ranch cook and baby sitter for Maury and Lucy. She wrote a book about the area. It was a great experience for both Maury and me.

The ranch has been bought by a very nice couple who raise quarter horses and who have renovated the old buildings and built a beautiful home several miles up the creek from the original place. Lucy had contacted them and they were kind enough to show us around and were anxious to hear Maury's and Lucy's recollections of the 'old days'.

On this trip I met Senator Alan Simpson in Cody. The Simpson family were old friends of Maury's mother and grandparents. I always admired him since the days of the confirmation hearings for Justice Clarence Thomas. I really appreciated his sense of humor-I wasn't disappointed.

THE CALIFORNIA ESCAPADE

We left for CA in mid August, 2013, trailing our pop-up camper. The trailer lights and brakes weren't working so we stopped by the dealer who sold it to us and the man twisted the connection and everything worked! We overnighted in a campground in Douglas WY. The next morning we had an accident while hitching the camper which resulted in a bad fall for me. We went to the emergency room-found no bones broken-just had bruises on my hip and leg. Should we turn back? Decided to go on with a prescription for pain and determination to forge ahead!

Arrived in Gillette, WY, to visit the son of a friend from high school days and my maid of honor at Jim's and my wedding in 1950. He was doing some interesting work in recovering gold from coal fly ash and Maury wanted to check it out. We spent 3 days there with him and his daughter. Made a short trip to Devils Tower, me limping and groaning most of the time.

We headed off for CA. About 75 miles out we discovered the trailer lights and brakes weren't working again so we limped into Casper and found a very nice couple running an RV repair shop. They took pity on us and repaired the problem while we waited. We took off and arrived in Happy Camp, CA, on the 4th day without any further trouble.

We spent a week there in a very nice campground-Maury prospecting and me resting up from the accident. Maury couldn't use any of his mining equipment due to new restrictions imposed by the State. We met many interesting people there-one, Dave McCracken, who owns the New 49ers' Club and many miles of claims on the Klamath River. He has written 4 books on mining and a biography. He gave a very interesting talk about his life as a Navy Seal and adventures. He had been to many of the same places I have looking for gold and gems while Jim and I were looking for black gold, oil.

A NEW FRIEND

We were introduced to the resident miner, Ken Phelps, an 87 year-old WW II Navy vet, recipient of the bronze star and 4 combat medals. He took a shine to Maury and me and imparted some of his years-long experience in gold prospecting to Maury.

Ken Phelps

Ken was a searchlight operator on a troop carrier. He could turn on his light only when so ordered. During the Battle of Okinawa he suffered permanent loss of hearing being 40 feet from where a Kamikase hit his ship. He survived because he got behind a gun turret. He spotted another Kamikase headed directly for him and, hoping to blind the pilot, he turned his searchlight on him. Just before hitting the ship the plane nose-dived into the sea. He "shot down" 4 more before it was over. He was called to the bridge and the Captain asked, "Who gave you the order to turn your light on?" "No one", he said, "I didn't have time to ask permission". An officer who observed all this through binoculars told Ken he didn't blind the pilots he fried them from the intense heat of the searchlight which was lit by an electric arc rod. When he checked his light the rod was almost all used up!

He had a twinkle in his eye when he told us the story but took us to his trailer and showed us the plaque his shipmates had given him for saving all hands except the 8 killed by the first Kamikase. He was 19 at the time. We have now shaken hands with a member of the finest generation.

We drove home after a week at Happy Camp with our pocket full of gold ($20 worth)

ABOUT THE "KIDS"

Meanwhile the grandkids are all grown up and leaving home.

Jessie and Cara have grown up to be such beautiful young ladies. Both were volley ball players in high school where they were rated MOST AGGRESSIVE! Maybe influenced by their hockey playing father and brothers. They both graduated from Fort Lewis College-Jessie Magna Cum Laude. Jessie now lives in Minnesota and is working in the hotel industry but longs to return to Colorado. Cara is getting her cosmetology license in Fort Lauderdale. She loves it there and doesn't miss Colorado at all. Jared is going to Gustavus Adolfus College in Minnesota. He still plays hockey and is still the family entertainment provider competing with his older brother, Sean, for the most outlandish sport stories.

Sean and Whitney are serving in the Air Force in California and working on their Masters Degrees.

Aislinn has done quite well in academics-earning a scholarship for college spending time studying in Australia and Israel. Seems she got the wanderlust from her Grandma!

And I am missing all of them and the good old days when they were growing up.

I even have a thirteen year old great granddaughter-Jada, Ryan's daughter. How can this be? Everyone's getting older and I'm staying the same!??

I'm still making jewelry and have started making earth angels and bird sculptures out of semi-precious rocks and stones. Ryan took pictures of them and they are in a file on one of Maury's thumb drives.

I still play bridge but drive my friends crazy for not learning all of the new conventions. My excuse: AGE-it comes in handy sometimes.

I usually send out Christmas letters to my friends each year and have been told they read like a TRAVELOGUE!

Maybe I've lived up to Maury's family's definition of me: 'A real trooper'. However, that's not how I'd like to be remembered. How about, 'I married adventure'! Thanks, Osa. I personally have already found my gold-my friends, my family, my God and, of course, my wonderful, crazy husband.

So darling, save the last dance for me!

Who knows what the future will hold for us-it's 2013 and we just might have a few years left.

We are both in our 80's and have to deal with various maladies-such as slowing down a bit and not hearing as well. One of my favorite stories deals with hearing loss. We attended a valentine's dance one year and Maury bought me 2 beautiful red roses at the party. Upon arriving home I put them in a favorite vase that had 3 tubes for flowers. I told Maury I needed another red rose. His reply was, "Why do you want a rib roast?" So much for communication.

I found this poem while reading the autobiography of Martha Black one of the pioneers of the Alaskan gold rush and I hope it applies to me.

Let me grow lovely growing old,
So many fine things to do.
Silks and ivory and gold,
And lace need not be new.

There is magic in old trees,
Old books a glamour hold.
Why not I as well as these,
Grow lovely growing old?

SOME OF THE PEOPLE IN THIS STORY

Grace Black Hammond and Maury Hammond
Jim Black
Karen - 1st daughter
Susan - 2nd daughter
Barbara - 3rd daughter
James III - 1st son
Claire - 4th daughter
John - 2nd son
Jean - Jim's sister
George - Jean's husband
Bob - Grace's brother
Betty Jane - Bob's wife
Ernie and Mollie Haynes - best friends
Isabel and Larry Littlefield - best friends
Peggy and Charley Wheeler - best friends
Rose and Bernie Texeira - best friends
Sharon and Charlie Wilmuth - best friends
Susan and Joe McKee - best friends
Linda and Jim Coapland - best friends
Al and Dee Deutsch - my favorite pastor and his wife
Ken Phelps - WW II Vet & prospector
Ryan - Karen's son

Sean - Claire's 1ˢᵗ son
Jesse - Claire's 1ˢᵗ daughter
Cara - Claire's 2ⁿᵈ daughter
Jared - Claire's 2ⁿᵈ son
Aislinn - Barbara's daughter
J.C. and Britney Dixon - John's step children
Jada - Ryan's daughter
Bengt Eld - Karen's 1ˢᵗ husband
Bill McLaughlin - Karen's second husband
Duncan Harding - Susan's husband
Nelson Betancourt - Barbara's husband
Mike Bertsch - Claire's husband
Cathy - John's 1ˢᵗ wife
Sally - Maury's 1ˢᵗ wife
Lucy - Maury's sister
Terry - Maury's 1ˢᵗ daughter
Audrey - Terry's daughter

SUMMERS; 2009, 2010 & 2011

There's gold and it's haunted & haunting
It's luring me on as of old
Yet it isn't the gold that I'm wanting
So much as just finding the gold.
(From Robert Service's "Spell of the Yukon")

These are my notes from 3 summers in Alaska. There will be some repetitions in my biography.

June 5, 2009   Off to Alaska!   Woodland Park-Vancouver

The Doctor's report before leaving for Alaska shows a tumor on my right kidney. Decided to go ahead with the trip & made an appointment with Dr Cohen in Pgh. Will probably have it removed there-50-50 chance of cancer. I'm banking on the better 50. Not a very good way to start a vacation, but I'm sure the good Lord will look after me. Told the kids about it but no one else beside Pat, my hair dresser, who promised not to tell anyone. She has been my confidant for 20 years. So, with that hanging over my head, I'm ready to go thru hell or high water After removing a large amount in the large suitcase so it was under 50lbs, we were on our way. Still had to pay $70 for 2 suitcases ea. The flt to Denver was smooth & we had a delay of 1 hr on the second leg to Portland. We made it in time for our Air Canada prop plane to Vancouver. Stayed at the Sheraton 4 Points. All was very nice except the martinis were watered down & the waitress said she couldn't serve a double in less than 2 hrs; Father Canada said so!

June 6   Vancouver

We slept late, had a cup of coffee & made our way to the Port at 12:00 noon. We had an Indian (India) with a head turban for our taxi ride. Huge amt of people boarding-looks like the ship is full. Found our cabin & one suitcase was already there. Explored the ship & ate a little while waiting for the lifeboat drill at 4:45. We then walked around the ship & stopped at the atrium. I bought 2 rings for $30 & we celebrated with martinis which Maury said were "up to snuff". Went to dinner with a short dance on the way. Sat at a table with 2 couples-one from Scotland-she did all of the talking. The other couple were from Idaho. Before dinner while at the atrium we met a very nice couple from S Fran just married 4 months. They were our age-we got their names & plan to contact them later. After dinner we made our way to the theater & both of us fell asleep during the comic act. Went to bed early & slept soundly till 8:00 AM.

June 7   At Sea

Didn't do much but lounge around. Evening was dress-up-had pictures taken. Ate dinner. Food was good but not great. The pictures came out just OK. Who were those 2 old folks?

June 8   Ketchican

Got off the ship & walked around town. Bought an ulu with a jade handle, some jade beads & another ulu with a bone handle. Had dinner with 2 interesting couples in the Blue Moon dining room. Went to a stage show. It was very good-great costumes & Maury went to sleep! Went to the totem village run by Tsimshian tribe. Took a taxi there & back-the Sourdough Line.

June 9   Juneau

Went to town & walked around till noon. Russell Shivers picked us up at the red dog Saloon. Went by to see his wife, Caroline, at her carpet shop. Had lunch at Donna's Hallibut & Chips. Drove up to the Mendenhall Glacier, to the salmon hatchery & out to see Russell's home. Met Opal, the dog with no tail, because of all the Lladro figurines sitting around. Russell dropped us back to the ship. Had a nice day-talking about old friends from Venezuela & sluice boxes!

June 10th, 11th & 12th   Skagway

Went by train to White Pass-left at 8:30-back at noon. Had a great lunch at a diner close to the ship-halibut again! We then walked about town. Pretty much all of the same stuff. Had a nice evening on board. Sailed to Glacier Bay. Saw some beautiful glaciers- Margery was the most beautiful. The weather was great & the scenery breathtaking.

Set sail for Prince Rupert Sound. It was pretty foggy. Saw orca & seals. Arrived Prince Rupert Sound. The weather wasn't good but we saw many salmon fishermen & on to College Fiord. Went to another musical & Maury fell asleep again.

Packed all of our things & stayed in our cabin all evening.

June 13   Whittier-Anchorage

Arrived in Whittier. Got off ship at 8:30. Bus to Anchorage. Saw plenty of bald eagles-one at the dock & another on the way to Anchorage also saw a moose & some mountain goats. Very nice trip-1 ½ hrs. Arrived at Princess Terminal & called Casey. He picked us up & took us to the hotel. Went shopping for flip-flops for Maury& had lunch at the Bears Tooth Saloon-had fish & garlic fries. We went back to the hotel & went to sleep early.

June 14   Anchorage-Tok

The rest of the crew arrived & we had breakfast with Glenn, Casey, Ron & Michael at the hotel. Did some last minute shopping for supplies & headed for Tok-took the wrong road. Had lunch in Palmer & arrived in Tok at 7:30 PM. Stayed at a motel there & got to Chicken the next day at 11:30.

June 15   Tok-Chicken

The road to Chicken was good-took only 2 hrs & we went slowly following Glenn's rig. Glenn & Casey decided to return to Tok & wait for the rest of the group driving up from the lower 48. They spent the night there &didn't arrive back until 2:30 PM. Ron, Michael, Maury & I took a tour of the "Pedro", a bucket gold dredge which was pretty interesting. Mike Busby bought it for $1.00 over near Fairbanks & had it hauled to Chicken. It moved quite a bit of gravel during the '30s & '40s.

The first night in Chicken Ron stayed in the extra bedroom in our apt. Michael had a cabin which was only available for one night. The apt was pretty nice-nothing fancy but it did have a sink running water. A king size bed in our bedroom & 2 twins in the 2nd bedroom for which they charged $60 for extra people. There was table & chairs, a 2-burner gas plate & a heater which we haven't needed. Showers downstairs-$3.00 for 3 minutes! The people who own the place, Lou & Mike Busby, seem nice. Lou was a bit grumpy when we checked in (change in reservations) but has softened up a bit. Set up our portable refrigerator & its working good.

June 16   Chicken-Mile Post 103 Taylor Hwy

Everyone was anxious to get to the claim on Uhler Creek as the surveyor was due there Thus night so they will set up camp tonight & tomorrow. Finally, at 12:00 Glenn showed up & said the rest of the crew should be here soon-they came at 2:30. The story was that Baltimore Jim had enough of travelling with the crew who said he was poking along refusing to go faster than 50 MPH so he parked his rig in Tok and thumbed a ride to Anchorage on his way south. The rest of them seemed in good spirits except having to go back & get the rig B Jim left in Tok.

At about 4:00 PM they got the show on the road & I went along to see the claim site. One truck broke down on the 2 hr drive to MP 103 Everything was unloaded on the side of the road so they could scout out the claim which was deemed to have a bad road in. It was quite a sight to see everyone unchain & drive the small equipment off the carriers. Glenn was the star of that show. Ron was all excited and tried to tell him how to do the job until Glenn asked "Ron, don't you have to pee or something?" After all this was finished it was about 8:30 PM.

Since they needed to get the loaded rig & Casey's wash plant in Tok, Grant, Casey, Michael, Maury & I headed back in Grant's 4-seater King Ranch pickup (Cowboy Cadillac). Me on part of Maury's lap & part on the seat. We made it back to Chicken in good time before Maury's leg was ruined. They dropped us off after getting some sandwiches at "Susan's Café" & went on their way to Tok. Maury & I tried to get a bite to eat but all was closed. So we had a piece of Susan's giant cinnamon roll & were in bed by 11:00.

June 17   Chicken

Around 1:00 AM Casey et al arrived back in Chicken & dropped off a coffee maker & toaster & went on their way to MP 103. Maury was so excited to get back to the claim he couldn't sleep. Tried to make coffee but, of course the electricity doesn't come on till 8:00 AM so he fiddled around until 3 or 4:00 AM & finally took off. It was still daylight. Don't think it ever gets dark.

June 18

After Maury left I went back to sleep & woke up around 8:30-had a good Community coffee & the rest of the cinnamon roll. Don't have any plans for today except reading & maybe a few games of solitaire. I'll be anxious to hear what the day brings for the 8 prospectors; Casey, Michael, Grant, Jerry, Tim, Glenn, Ron & Maury. They are all so excited & took care with their language when I was around-I'm sure a major accomplishment in the annals of "North to Alaska" miners! Believe me, it was a great experience for me & they were all great to me even though I was probably a "wet blanket". Of course that didn't keep me from giving them a few suggestions here & there which they accepted in good "Grace".

Maury arrived around 9:30-too late for a shower-took a sponge bath-& we went over to the Chicken Bar where I bought 1 ½ sandwiches & a cinnamon bun for $14.50! Maury had to show the young bartender how to make a martini. Came back to the apt & Maury was asleep as soon as his head hit the pillow.

They got into the claim & found all sorts of machinery & food left from the owner, Louie Schene who had died in Jan 2009 & his brother, Adrian, who died in Dec 2008.

I met a couple, "Jones", who were from N Carolina & had relatives in WP-Hatten & Jarvis, one of whom had been choir director at the Methodist Church!

June 19

After Maury left I went back to sleep & woke at 9:30-looked out the window & saw the big black pickup. Maury & Ron had come back to town to talk to the BLM people & were happy things went well-got BLM's OK to start mining. They stayed for breakfast & headed back at 12:45. Things are going well at the claim. They found a cat that had stowed away in their cargo trailer in Whitehorse & is now the camp pet named "Hitch".

A quiet afternoon-washed my hair in the sink-don't think I've done that in a long time. Went over to Susan's & bought a hamburger plus a cup & T-shirt for Jada & a couple of pens. It's been a rainy day & windy. Saw a helicopter fly over. The BLM was supposed to check the claim by air. Hope they are OK at the claim. Maury didn't come in tonight-guess they are having a good time. Read "Devil Went to Austin" till the light got too dim-that was 11:00 PM.

June 20

Got up & had some of Maury's coffee & a blueberry muffin from Susan's café. Read some of my book & took a long shower-a $3.00 one! Fell like a new person. The weather seems nice-a little overcast, but blue skies mostly.

Maury came in late-10:00 PM. I had a corned beef sandwich from the café for him-everything was closed except the outhouse. I asked for ice this afternoon & all they had was a gallon jug of frozen water. We drained the water off & made martinis by shaking the gin over the ice-not bad-that was my idea-I never cease to amaze myself-must be my pioneer experience!

Maury finally got to take a shower. I thought I was going out to the claim but Maury didn't think it was a good time as Keener (geologist) was there to assess the gold possibilities. We went over to Sue's café for breakfast. The breakfast sandwich was more than I could eat. Sue was her same harassed self-expecting a bus load of people in. She had cin rolls baking-said she didn't get any sleep because her mom was ranting all night. The tourists came in & they were buying-lots of stuff from her shop. I think that is where the gold is. Maury bought a bottle of tequila for the Timroth clan & left at 8:00 AM. I will finish my book & play another 100 games of solitaire. I was so cold after Maury left I finally decided to get into bed to keep warm-woke up at 11:45! Went over to Sue's place-bought a pencil & 2 pr of Alaska socks to send to Dad & a reindeer brat for Maury's dinner. Bought some soup at the chicken Outpost & ate a little of it saving the rest for Maury's dinner. Surprise! Maury came in at 6:00 PM-followed Ron & Jerry who needed to get their RV serviced-water, etc. They weren't able to get propane-said that was in Tok. Maury needed to charge his computer so I baby sat that while he went to the apt to fix a drink-in the process he dumped the $4.95 soup in the sink by mistake. Talked to Michael for awhile. No gold so far-everyone panned 8-10 pans. Not a good sign. Keener mapped out some sites for them & they will set up the sluice boxes tomorrow. Came back to the apt & Maury ate his dinner-early to bed-oh yes, he lost his belt when he unstrapped his gun so he is now wearing a yellow cord for a belt! He is looking more & more like an old gold miner-hasn't shaved & is looking pretty scruffy-still loveable though! He doesn't want me to go out to camp yet as he will be the guy to set up the sluice boxes since they are his design. Afraid a bear will get me while he's working-I wonder if there isn't a cub out there wearing a belt with a Texas longhorn buckle.

Sunday, June 21st
    Father's day-bought a card for Maury:

            It's written in the stars and whispered in the wind
            Destiny would guide our hearts to a love that knows no end

Maury left at 6:00. I went back to bed-what else should I do? Woke up at 9:30! Went down to take my "Sunday" shower" but there was a couple waiting who just drove in-looked like Bonny & Clyde-decided to let them go ahead of me! Got Maury a hamburger at Sue's-he didn't arrive until 10:00 PM. I had a chicken salad sandwich. He was pretty tired-didn't get as much done as he expected on the sluice boxes. Said Casey was becoming a really good hand. Keener picked out 7 spots to dig & Ron will have the last word on where to start.

    The longest day-didn't know they could get any longer. Never have seen darkness yet! Sue agreed to get 14 bags of ice in Tok for our crew-should be ready by 6:00 PM. She was quite talkative this AM. She must have quite a story to tell. She's from Philadelphia originally. Everyone here knows about the Schene claims (Uhler Creek) & every story is different. She said all of the miners are a little crazy-so is that what I have to look forward to? Maury said the guys spend half of their time looking for things. I found his belt hanging in the bedroom closet-he couldn't figure out how it got there. Osmosis maybe!

Monday June 22

After coffee & scones, we went for gas & water. Ron & Jerry had asked for cat food & litter-don't know where they thought that could be found. Maury left at 10:00. Sent mail to John & Mo this AM to let them know we are OK & still sane? The cleaning lady knows all about Louie Schene too-said he was a real character. He was a university graduate geologist. Everyone seemed to like him but he was pretty much a hermit. She also knew Wade (Wade Creek)-said he shot himself because his life was over. Walked around & took pictures today. Asked Lou about laundry-she said one word-Tok! Guess that's it. Finished the book, "Martha Black"-what a great story, a real pioneer & smart lady.

Tuesday June 23

Went with Maury to the claim. Arrived with 14 bags of ice that Gary (works for Susan at Chicken café) bought in Tok. No one was up at the RV. The 1 hr drive–7 miles off the main road was pretty bad-bumpy & slow. We arrived finally & things were stirring. Michael was doing his wash. The rest were getting ready for the day. Most of the equipment was downstream about 1 mile where they were going to test Casey's wash plant. We had coffee & waited for Ron to arrive-the big kahuna. There were several tents where each (Michael, Casey & Tim) had their sleeping bags. The groceries were in a big building. There were other buildings, a freezer, an old Maytag washing machine & a myriad of bottles & cans the Schenes had saved. A couple of pickup trucks-license plates '71, a dozer & lots of other equipment-that alone were pretty valuable. We stayed in the main tent while the others came & went to start up the operation. Tim was welding legs for the hopper. He is quite a character-white beard-sort of an old time philosopher-an excellent mechanic-worked for Glenn in Basalt, CO. Finally word came back that there was discord at the site so we all went down there in the ranger, a 4-wheel ATV, Ron, Maury & I. Over streams, rocks & rills-took lots of pictures. They finally resolved their problems-probably too many chiefs & no Indians. We came back & got lists of things they needed in Tok as we are going there tomorrow to get our laundry done & buy a few supplies for the apt. After a bumpy ride back we went to bed early. After Maury got filled up with gas the truck wouldn't start so I waited at Sue's & got reindeer brats & cherry pie for our dinner.

Wed June 24   Chicken-Tok-Chicken

Got up & since the truck wouldn't start Mike (Busby) finally agreed to give us a jump. We were on our way to Tok at 8:00 AM-took us 1 hr & 15 mins but Maury was driving too fast. Hit a crow & seemed too happy?? We arrived in Tok found a laundromat & I got all of the clothes in 4 washers. We then went to the Chevron station where Maury met Henry who became his new best friend. They decided the car needed a new alternator & could get it installed there. I went back to finish the clothes & finished all when Maury came back with the truck. Henry had introduced him to Bonnie Achman at the Jack Wade Gold Co. who had a lot to tell about her adventures in the region. She had been in AK since 1966 married a miner & they struck it rich-had a huge gold nugget weighing 56 ¾ oz now worth over $45,000 as bullion (56.75 x 800 fine x $1000). She turned down $200,000 for it as a collector's piece. Maury took me there to meet Bonnie & we had a nice conversation. She gave me some gold mining advice. Called Claire & Karen on my cell phone & Maury called Mo. We left there & had lunch at Fast Eddie's-had a nice lunch & went to the grocery store-the only one in Tok. Bought supplies-spent over $750 on camp supplies & our bill was $129.00 (camp supplies included food, cigarettes & whiskey!). By the time we finished we were both exhausted. Maury was completely out of sorts since he really doesn't like shopping of any kind. We stopped at the Visitor Center to check on transportation to Fairbanks on the July 4-no luck-could only get there on the 3rd. So that means 1 extra night in Fairbanks since our plane leaves on the 5th at 9:30 AM. Arrived back in the apt at 7:30 PM. Maury had a spoonful of peanut butter & I had ½ of one of Sue's huge cookies. We were both exhausted-I always thought shopping was therapeutic-not so! Went to bed early.

Thu June 25

Maury left at 6:00 AM. Couldn't wait to get back to the claim to see what was going on& to deliver groceries to everyone. I tried to go back to bed but it was freezing. I forgot & left the window open. Had some crazy dream about Susan-caught her & Karen smoking & told her she should stop-she told me I should stop drinking martinis with Maury. I woke trying to figure it all out. Made egg salad for tonight & did my hair-a major undertaking with the mirror propped up on an empty box-quite an invention if I do say so! It looks pretty good! Read some more of Mark Levin's "Liberty and Tyranny"-I can only take it in small doses-pretty good stuff-called "A Conservative Manifesto". He is called "The Great One" by Rush. Maury arrived at 7:30 with tales of discord at the camp. Seems Grant is on everyone's—t list. But he's the son of one of the big investors, Jerry Timroth, Ron's brother. So that poses a problem. He has managed to tick everyone off somehow.

On his way back out to MP 103. Maury met Jim Schene (Adrian's son & owner of the Uhler claims) who was on his way to the claim with an Indian woman, probably an Eskimo, her husband & a dog. Talked to them quite a while. Also had to stop for a family of ptarmigans crossing the road. Met mark Breece at 103. He's camped on the ridge south of 103. He goes 15 miles on a 4-wheeler to his claim on Napoleon Creek (a tributary of the South Fork of the Forty Mile River upstream of Uhler) & walks the last ¼ mile. Stays for the summer suction dredging. He is expecting his girl friend for the 4th of July. So Ron & Jerry & Grant will have neighbors (they are in a motor home at103).

Lou brought a letter from Zana, Ron's wife. She even smiled. We had our egg salad sandwiches & potato chips-tasted pretty good.

Fri June 26

Went up to see the postmistress today-mail comes in Tue & Fri. She was very nice-quite talkative. We were there to check on a part coming in for Tim & it wasn't there yet. Her name is Robin Hammond. She & her husband have bid on the Schene claims-supposedly $50,000 or more. So being old timers they must know something about them. I got 2 parcel post boxes to send some books back to CO. I'm also sending my jewelry & pastels back-I never did anything with them-I did try one pastel pic but gave up-it's been so long. I guess I'm out of practice. The buses come in from Dawson City carrying people from the cruise ships.

Maury arrived about 8:30. We had macaroni & cheese, crackers, cheese & salami. It has rained all day & is pretty cold in the apt. We started up the heater & it worked well. Still not much success at the claim. The visitors stayed the night & were cleaning up the cabin & burning trash left behind by their uncle Earl ("Louie"). Had 2 women & 3 men. Don't know what they brought for food. Maury is beginning to look like Grizzly Adams.

A note about the town of Chicken & surrounding area: there was a huge fire in 2004 & the scenery was devastated-some 2000 sq mi was burned. It is pretty around here-the fire came very close. There are several ponds & 2 or 3 troughs for gold panning gravel from Busby's claim. Flecks of gold are found. There are 20-30 RVs every night some huge ones-traveling hotels-even some tents. The café closes at 8:00 PM. There is a very nice gift shop there & you can get soup, sandwiches, ice cream, scones, coffee & cold sodas. Up the road is Sue's place-a bar, gift shop-not as fancy as the one here, a restaurant-mainly sandwiches, soup & some dinners-chicken, good hamburgers-very expensive. She has 2 or 3 Holland –America buses there every day. The third place in Chicken is "The City of Chicken". They have gas, a gift shop, some cabins & FLUSH TOILETS! Maury gets water & gas there for camp. That's about it-some hiking trails, an airstrip & Post Office. The days are long-thank heavens I brought some books. I wouldn't stay here again. The Busbys are unfriendly & not too helpful especially Lou who seems to barely tolerate us.

Sat June 27

Fried bacon this AM. It's amazing what you can do with 1 pan! Made coffee & toast. Maury left around 7:30. He's taking gas, water & ice back to camp. Our expenses are mounting. Maury has to pay $50 a round trip for gas to the claim & food is ridiculously high. Oh well-I guess we'll get it back someday when Maury gets his 4% of the gold! So far I think that's around $4.50! Maury stopped at the store & I ran over to give him the letter he forgot for Ron! I'm reading "Tisha" the story of a young teacher who came to Chicken in 1927. A true story & very well written. Maury came in late & we had cheese & crackers, tomato & 1 boiled egg. All of the places were closed as usual-I should be losing weight but don't think I am. The Schene family invited the miners for dinner. They had a memorial service for Louie & his brother, Adrian, & dumped their ashes in the little stream (pup as they are called in AK) by the cabin. Ron said a few words & it was appreciated by the family. A rainbow ended the service.

Sun June 28

We got up early & I decided to go out to the claim. We arrived at MP 103 at 7:45. The Timroths were stirring in their motor home. We went down to the claim & the Schenes were still there-Jim, Louie's nephew, his wife, Irene (Eskimo), their son, Jim, Jr, their adopted daughter (Eskimo) & her boyfriend who was much older. They were all very friendly & had cleaned out Louie's cabin & burned a lot of stuff. Adrian gave Ron permission to use all that was there & gave him an extension on his option to buy the claims till August 15th. They loaded up 3 pickups with stuff & took a Willys jeep, an old 1957 pickup, that started right up! (thanks to Tim). They left around 11:00 AM. I went up to the cabin to help cleanup & move things around so Ron, Jerry & Grant could move down from the motor home 1 hr away. I've never seen so much stuff-lots of books & everything imaginable under the sun. Don't think Louie & Adrian ever threw anything away. Michael & I worked for several hrs & it was still full of stuff! Michael burned a lot of things & we packed up the things that wouldn't burn & put them in a shed. There is a decent kitchen with a gas stove, microwave & cupboards full of cooking utensils & everything else you could think of. Maury, Glenn & Casey were across the creek trying to set up Louie's wash plant & finally got it going but not to their satisfaction.

We headed back around 5:00 PM & had to remove a fallen tree off the road. It was quite a sight watching Ron & Maury tug on the tree which almost got the best of them. Got back to Chicken at 7:15-all was closed so we had scrambled egg sandwiches, cheese, tomatoes, & onions-tasted pretty good. Maury had a $50 bottle of Bombay Sapphire gin so we drowned our sorrows & went to bed. I woke at 2:30 & Maury was up reading about operating a sluice box so he would have some pointers for tomorrow. Finally got him back to bed & I woke at 7:30. He was dressed & ready to go! Tomorrow is mail day & I'm sending some things out so we won't have so much weight. We will leave some things here (at camp).

Mon June 29

Here it is Monday & we leave Fri. Saw Mike Busby & he was very friendly-actually stopped me & asked how I was. Can't say I'm looking forward to the next week or so but it has to be done. I'm sure Maury hates to leave the guys but he insists on coming with me &, hopefully, he can come back soon. Went over to Sue's place & bought a new book, some T-shirts for the kids & 2 reindeer brat dinners. Fixed some dirty rice to go plus some ice cream for dessert. Couldn't get Lou to part with an envelope to send Power of Attorney to Zana so I made one & they did allow me to use scotch tape to finish it off. Looked pretty good-maybe if all else fails, I can go into the envelope making business!

Maury came in at 8:00 and they finally found GOLD! Got the sluice box working & thought they had about $250 worth. We figured Maury's share would be worth about $10. Oh well, just look at the fun they are having. Maury went to bed with a smile on his face!

Tue June 30

We slept late-6:30 & got ready to take the packages up to the mail. Sent 2 to Duncan & 1 to Dad with a present for Jada included. Better tell Karen to look out for it. Robyn was very nice-quite talkative & told us a little about herself. Maury asked if they in fact wanted to buy the Schene property & she said they were on the list! Looks like everyone is interested-probably has $300,000 in stuff (buildings & equipment) not counting the gold! Maury took off at 8:30 & here I am with my stale coffee & toast. I'm starting to get addicted to toast with peanut butter & orange marmalade. Lou arrived with a pkg for Tim & a Father's day card from Terry. I went over at 5:10 to get ice & selected 2 T-shirts for the kids. Fixed the rest of the rice w/the leftover reindeer brat & made some egg salad with the last 2 eggs. Saw Mike today carrying toilet paper to the outhouse & he said his job description had changed. Maury arrived later & said he helped start up the sluice with Glenn & then helped Casey who was overwhelmed with work (gold cleanup). Seems Casey gets any job that needs done. Don't know how long he will hold up under pressure. He is a nice kid and has a high boiling point which is a good thing-always has a smile & hug when he sees you. He's looking scraggly with a beard a hair flying. We were in bed by 10:30-still haven't seen any dark night yet-pretty much stays daylight all of the time. Ron, Jerry & Grant moved down to Louie's cabin so the motor home may not be used for the rest of the summer as it can't get down to Uhler Creek. Maury said it is a much better arrangement with everyone in one place.

Wed July 1

Today I'm going to try to get things together that we want to leave in AK so Maury can take them to Uhler Creek tomorrow. Started a new book, "The Final Frontiersman" interesting but not a woman's book-I'm sure M would like it. Also looked at the AAA Tour Book to see what is in Fairbanks (we will be spending July 4th there). Everyone is going on Fri to Tok with us so I guess they all need a day in town. M came in late-9:00 & we went up to Sue's saloon. Talked to Jamie Detchmendy who was bartending. Said he is a percussionist working in Austin on 6th St. Seems like a nice kid. Maury had his martini & I had a beer-$21. We came back to the apt & had our sandwiches that I got earlier in the day. Tried to get a cold beer for M when he came home but they wouldn't sell me one to take off the premise. We packed up everything we wanted to leave at Uhler Creek & got to bed at 11:00. No water tonight- place is full-looks like at least 45-50 campers-guess the recession hasn't hit the road folks.

Thus July 2

Slept till 6:30. M loaded up the coffee pot, toaster & freezer-forgot one box with leftover groceries in the pan & skillet. I filled his thermos, "The Great Stanley", last night so he had coffee (warm). I went over & got a cup from Mike who was doing books. Saw a very interesting mini sluice they were selling-should have gotten one for the claim. Well, maybe next time. Sent my coat, hat jeans, etc, to be kept till next year. Hope I make it! Picked up a book by Robt. K Tannenbaum called "Corruption of Blood" about another investigation of the Kennedy assassination-so far unsolved. Today should be pretty quiet-yesterday was beautiful & it looks like today will be the same. I've been sneezing since yesterday-lots of cotton from the trees floating around. I'm sure it's an allergy. Lou delivered 2 boxes that arrived from Anchorage. I guess mail is 1 day early because Fri is a holiday so I won't be able to send another pkg via parcel post. Guess I'll cram it in my suitcase somehow. Spent the evening at Sue's. Had a great salmon dinner & she paid for the drinks. Her Mother, Eleanor, sat with us & is quite a gal. We heard about all of the locals- most of whom Sue said were "A Hs" She has 2 sons, Wolfgang & Max & she lives in Fairbanks after the season is over. Sue said to be sure to talk to Judd Edgerton (mines on Napoleon Creek)-he would set you straight. All the others are thieves! The whole crew will be in tomorrow morning & plan to go to Tok-the cupboard is bare & we are ready to go.

Fri July 3   Chicken-Tok-Fairbanks

Goodbye Chicken! The whole crew arrived around 9:30 & we were on our way to Tok. Left Chicken without remorse. Lou didn't even say goodbye. Arrived in Tok @ 11:30. We all had lunch together-M & I left on the shuttle at 2:45 on to Fairbanks. Michael on to Anchorage. Had a nice trip to F'banks & arrived there about 6:30. The shuttle dropped us off at our hotel, Aspen Lodge. After getting settled we walked ½ mile or so to Pike's Landing &

got a seat outside by the Chena River-it was hot-had fish & chips. Walked over to the hotel which is where Ron, Michael & Maury stayed last Sept. We had an ice cream cone "Caribou Caramel" & flagged down a Taxi to take us back to Aspen Lodge. Tried to set up a riverboat tour but the office was closed. So we watched Fox News the first TV since we got to Chicken. Found out M Jackson died & Obama was leading us into destruction, also, Sarah Palin had resigned as Governor. Fell asleep with the TV on.

Sat July 4   Fairbanks

Had a nice breakfast. Awoke in time to call the tour & walked down to the pier to catch it at 9:45. Boarded the riverboat, a paddle wheeler, & it was a great trip down the Chena River-levee-beautiful homes-stopped to watch a demo of sled dogs & on to an Indian village which was quite nice. There were a lot of people on the tour; around 250. Got back in time to get a bite of lunch & off to the El Dorado Gold Mine by bus tour. Boarded a train to the mine area to see a demo of gold mining as its done today. Then on to the water troughs with our little pokes of pay dirt to pan them out. We got about $40 worth of gold between us & M bought me a locket into which they put about 2/3 of our gold. They served FREE cookies & coffee & had a huge gift shop. I managed to get away without buying anything! After arriving at the hotel, we had dinner there & were exhausted. Went to bed early & woke up at 3:00 AM.

Sun July 5   Fairbanks-Pittsburgh

Decided to pack up & were ready in <u>plenty</u> of time for the shuttle at 8:30 AM. No problem with the plane-cost $40 each for luggage. It was a 4 ½ hr flight to Minneapolis-called Claire & everyone else in the family & then on to Pgh-arrived at 10:00 PM. There was a 4 hr time difference from F'banks, so it was actually 6:00 PM AK time. Bob was there to meet us & we sat up a talked till 1:30 AM.

Mon July 5   Pittsburgh

Big day-Dr's appt at 10:30-didn't see Dr Cohen till 11:30 at which time he said he could do the operation but wanted to see the film from the CAT scan. So I had to call WP hospital & ask them to send it. Spent the rest of the day doing various tests-blood work, chest X-rays & EKG. Had lunch at Max's German restaurant. Made an appointment to see a GP tomorrow at 10:00 & waiting a time for a cardiologist-then will see Dr Cohen on Wed. Called everyone with the report-not much to tell-sorry someone didn't think about the CAT scan. I wanted to take another one but Dr Cohen said the insurance probably wouldn't pay. So they & just about everyone else were a pain in the ass! Went back to Bob's igloo & went to bed around 12:00.

Tue July 7

Got up & ready for & ready for my 10:00 appt to see Dr Abbey Spencer. She was very nice-said there was a problem w/EKG test & she would suggest a cardiologist. She called &got me an appt Mon at 9:00. I decided to call Dr Lane & have them send the last EKG & also the results of the stress test I had taken back in 2003. Bob went to pick up Amanda & family. They arrived & we had a hectic evening-3 little ones-quite a crew.

Wed July 8

Finally got straightened away & after breakfast, went to Wall Mart with the gangbuster crew-what an experience-glad I don't have that job. Ate lunch at Bob Evans. Took the wrong road back & ended up in Beaver Falls! On the way back, Marge (Cohen's nurse) called & said I should see a new doctor for my gall bladder operation on the 17th. I said I wasn't interested in gall bladder surgery I just wanted the kidney operation. She said she would cancel the appt. I'm pretty disappointed at the thought of a long drawn out recovery. I asked to speak to Cohen-don't know if he'll call or not.

Thu July 9

Took the crew to the zoo-had a great time-got home around 3:00 & I took a nap! Called the Dr's office to make sure I had a Wed appt. Marge finally called back at 3:30-was her usual bitchy self. Bobby, my nephew, & family came in around 6:30. We had dinner & they packed so they could leave early tomorrow. Sat up & talked till 1:30 AM.

Fri July 10

The house is quiet! The Maze family got away around 7:45 for their 1-week cruise-a major undertaking. I cleaned up & straightened up some & then M & I took off to get him a haircut. Stopped at Soergels & bought a few things-couldn't get pistachio ice cream-guess we'll have to settle for Ben & Jerrys. We'll head out later in search of ice cream& a place to get my hair done.

Sat July 11

Didn't do much today-rode around trying to get our bearings-got semi lost several times. Got our pics developed at Walgreens. Will wait till I get mine off the camera & then put them in albums. Ate at Applebees.

Sun July 12

Called Peggy my old high school friend-she could hardly believe it was me-made plans to get together after I have my Wed appt. Came home & fixed pot roast.

Mon July 13

Appt at 9:00-Carlton Cardiology-spent 4 ½ hrs there-stress test & echo cardiogram. Dr Said Ismail (a woman) who was born in Bagdad & educated in England & Ireland changed my blood pressure meds. She said the tests showed enlarged heart & that the left ventricle wasn't working normally which slowed down the heart muscles. Oh well, what next? By the time I'm thru with this, I'll probably find out I'm lucky to be alive! Ate lunch at Max's German restaurant finally at 2:00 PM. Came home & rested up from all the exercise-the stress test was chemical-no running on the machine which was better for me since my leg has been bothering me some. It was a strange sensation-the chemical did the work-my reaction was minimal.

Tue July 14

Work day-laundry & waiting to see what Dr Cohen has to say. Amy called & will be in Thurs night.

Wed July 15

Got to Dr Cohen's office at 1:20 for a 1:40 appt-finally saw him at 4:00! The news was bad-he said it was necessary to remove the entire kidney-also I should get the gall bladder out. I was dumb struck & couldn't even think of any questions to ask. We went from there to Aladdin's restaurant-Lebanese food-just OK. Called everyone & gave them the news. Still have to see the other doctor about the gall bladder surgery. That will slow things down quite a bit. Marge will make an appt & call me tomorrow.

Thu July 16

Finally, at 11:30 Marge called. I won't be able to see Dr Young until the 24th & that will mean no operation until Dr Cohen comes back from vacation-Aug 8! She was her usual nasty self & I finally had to tell her so. We made arrangements to go to FL on the 28th & come back Aug 9. May go to see Terry & Andrew in eastern PA next week for a few days.

Sun July 19

Since we will need to wait till the 24th to see Dr Young, we decided to go to Allentown & on to Riverside as soon as Bob gets back from the cruise. They arrived Saturday & we left today.

Wed, Jul 22

Had a nice visit with Terry, Andrew & Fred, the parrot who immediately bit Maury. Andrew is parrot crazy & I expect him to be trained by Fred soon. We stayed 2 nights & went on to see Lucy (Maury's sister). Spent 1 night there. Had a great lobster dinner-took Julie (Lucy's granddaughter) to the beach & aquarium-drove into NYC to see Audrey, Had dinner & got back late to Riverside-Lucy drove. Got back to Pgh pretty tired.

Fri, July 24

Finally, got to see Dr Young & he was the exact opposite of Dr Cohen who is no- nonsense-very likeable-explained everything. He said he would work with Dr Cohen to remove the gall bladder as soon as the kidney was removed. He's an amateur geologist & has cattle farms so he & Maury hit it off quite well.

Sat, July 25

Had a 3 hr lunch with Peggy & Randy. Promised to keep in touch.

Sat, Aug 8

Returned from 10 days in FL to see Dad-mainly helping Karen get ready for her move to Ryan's. Found Dad in pretty good shape-he got his TV programmed so he can watch the ball games.

Mon, Aug 10

Operation day! Woke up from the anesthesia in ICU-I was to spend 1 day there-ended up from Mon to Thu (actually 1:30 AM Fri) when they moved me to a semi-private room. Was discharged Sat noon. All went well with the surgery. The Kidney was removed-the cancerous tumor was entirely contained in the kidney with benign borders. Met with Dr Cohen-he said, "Congratulations, you're cured!" Thank God for that & the many good thoughts & prayers of many family & friends. Recovery slow but am getting stronger every day

Tue, Sept 1   Pittsburgh-Woodland Park

Three weeks from surgery we head back driving Bobby's car to CO. Left Sun, Aug 30 @ 10:15 AM.

Arrived WP at 4:00 PM Tue, Sept 1. We stopped in St Louis to see Susan & Joe McKee-Susan still caring for Joe after 40 years. Joe is slowly deteriorating & is in independent living at a near-by nursing home. What a gal that Susan is-surely a candidate for Sainthood.

Cathy brought groceries, Claire & Mike came, Claire brought a bouquet of beautiful sunflowers! We talked & got caught up on all the WP goings on. Had unpacked earlier & went thu some of our mail.

So good to be home!

SUMMER 2010

June 7, 2010

Off to Alaska again this time in a 30 ft RV equipped with a TV, microwave, oven & toilet! Pulled by Maury's new pickup a 2006 Ford F-250. Got an early start only to be delayed due to no electrical connection between truck & trailer-no lights or brakes. After about 6 trips between Gateway & Phil Long Ford the problem was finally solved-it was bad wiring on the pickup. Got away from the Springs at 2:15 PM after debating whether we should go home & start over. Got thru Denver early rush hour traffic & made it to Cheyenne, WY, for our 1st night on the road.

Had a restful night after all the trauma & went on to Columbus, MT, for the 2nd night. We were getting pretty good at parking & setting up the RV by now. The people at Columbus asked if Maury had been a truck driver-he did so well parking the RV. We went thru Canadian customs without any problem-Maury declared the "big bear gun" and had all the proper papers so that wasn't a problem. The 3rd night we stayed at Fort McCloud & the next, 4th, night at McCloud Lake Resort. The 5th night at Bucking Horse Resort, the 6th at Watson Lake & the 7th at Carmacks where the light came on to check the engine. We went on to Dawson & decided to get a hotel room-hot shower & a night (8th) on the town at Diamond Tooth Lil's. We had dinner at Sourdough Joe's-halibut-very good. The show was great & we sat at a table with folks from BC. We got the pickup serviced & were on our way to Uhler via the Top of The World Highway.

June 16   Mile Post 103 Taylor Highway

Arrived 103 midday. Parked the camper & headed down to camp on Uhler Creek. The road was pretty bad & we got about 1/3rd of the way & got stuck. About the time Maury decided we may spend the night or he would walk about 5 miles to camp, along came Cody & Ron in the Marooka (a half-track dump truck) & pulled us out. We went back to 103 where we spent the night. Ron came up the next morning & asked if we wanted to pull the camper down. That seemed like an impossible task so we declined.

June 17   Fairbanks

We drove to Fairbanks to pick up Michael & do some grocery & parts shopping for the camp. We stayed at Pikes landing.

June 18   Fairbanks-Tok-103

After Michael arrived we spent the next day shopping at Wall Mart, Sam's & Fred Meyer, a huge store with <u>everything</u>. We left completely loaded, ice parts & stopped in Tok for a few more items. Arrived around midnight at 103. Saw a beautiful sunset. Maury did all the driving. They dropped me off at the camper & Maury took Michael down to Uhler & got back to 103 around 4:00 Am.

June 20

Jerry, Grant and Jim had arrived safely. We took the camper to Tok for service & repairs. We stopped in Chicken to check on Josie who was to come on Tues. We went on to Tok, ate at Fast Eddie's, got the RV serviced and did some laundry. Stopped at Wade gift shop while in Tok & Maury bought me a beautiful nugget pendant with a white sapphire. Talked to Bonnie Achman. Maury also opened a bank account in Tok. We stopped in Chicken to make sure Josie would be coming to install HughesNet-sounds like she couldn't come till Thus. We paid her $375 appointment fee. On our way back, we stopped at Walker Fork Campground to check on moving there. They have good facilities and a Camp Manager-wife couple who seemed quite nice. The length of stay was only 1 week but could be extended. It rained again; the truck and RV looked like chocolate bars!

While in Chicken, we picked up the mail and had a long talk with Robin Hammond and she said to make sure we all come in for the big 4th of July picnic. We made it back to 103 and Grant arrived with water and gas cans & back we went to Chicken to fill them. We met a couple at Sue's who were writing for "The Milepost" (a large detailed annual Alaskan cruise & travel guide book). She was from Palmer and he from Greeley. It had rained all night again & we were getting pretty disgruntled with the stay at 103 & pretty much decided to move to the campground at Walker Fork-about 30 minutes away from 103.

June 21   MP 101-Uhler Creek

At 10:30 we were having coffee@ breakfast & the crew arrived from camp & said they were going to load our RV onto Glenn's flat bed trailer. They (Cody, Aaron, Jim, Jerry, Grant and the Hauler-in-Chief, Glenn) got the RV loaded & secured to the flatbed which was pulled by the dump truck. The road was terrible and I had my doubts that we could make it. They got within one mile of camp & stopped-decided to swap the dump truck for a dozer the next AM to negotiate 9 switchbacks which are pretty tight. We spent the night there on a slanted road-slept fairly well even though our feet were going downhill. We were so tired by then it didn't matter too much.

June 22   Uhler Creek

Maury and I drove down to camp and the RV arrived safely with only a few scratches. It was unloaded and put in place among a stand of trees about 200 feet from the quiet little stream which we hoped would hold riches in gold for all. Cody wrote on the side of the camper thru the dirt: "Gold or Bust" that stayed on till washed off by more rain. The "Gang" were pretty proud of themselves with good reason-it was quite an accomplishment & Glenn got a big hug from yours truly.

June 25   Uhler

Started mining (Ron had bought a new washplant, table & jig in Brighton, CO, which took several weeks to put together). I slept in late and busied myself putting things away. Michael and Maury put up a tent on one end of the RV to store things that we couldn't keep in the camper. So Maury had another garage to fill up! Maury went up to the Command Center (CC), Louie's cabin, & that night I fixed dinner and we watched an old Flip Wilson program.

June 26   Uhler

More rain! Awoke with a bad pain-think I have a U.T. infection-drank lots of water and took aspirin. We got the RV heater working. Maury went up to the CC to see what was going on-didn't return till 2 AM. They were celebrating getting all of the machinery working!

June 27   Uhler-Fairbanks

Still having some pain. Maury said they needed some things in Fairbanks so he volunteered to go & take me along to see a doctor. After a big Sunday breakfast of Raisin Bran we left at 12:30. Every bump on the road was painful. We arrived in Tok and met Henry and Dana for dinner. Arrived Fairbanks at 10:30-couldn't find a room-finally stayed at Alpine Lodge where we stayed last year. Couldn't get them down to a reasonable rate so we paid $200 a night there-it did include breakfast.

June 28   Fairbanks-Tok

Got up early and Maury dropped me off at the clinic and took off to do the camp shopping. The clinic was very nice and I didn't have to wait long to see the Dr Lee Ann. I took a urine sample but they wanted a new one. I spent 1 ½ hrs trying to fill the cup and then finally got the results, a U.T. infection! They gave me a prescription to fill at Walmart and I called Maury. He had done most of the shopping by then and came to pick me up. Someone had gashed the side of the truck while he was parked at Walmart and he had a white dot on the back of his new shirt-something had dripped down on him (lots of pigeons flying around). I told him I guess I couldn't let him off on his own again! We filled the prescription, finished shopping and ate lunch at the Pump House (originally used to house large pumps to pump water out of the Chena River over a ridge to the placer mines several miles away). Checked out of the hotel and made our way back to Tok, 4 1/2 hours. Arrived at 10:30 PM. Stayed at Tok Motel the only place available in Tok. Had coffee and pie at Fast Eddie's.

June 29   Tok-Eagle-Summit

Got up the next AM and bought a few groceries for our RV and made our way to Chicken. Stopped at Sue's for lunch and made our way to 103. Stopped & met Cecil & Judy Cox (miners) at their camp at MP 85 on Jack Wade Creek. Quite a place. Cecil's an American

Indian from OK. Their camp was pretty bad - dirty and messy. They offered us a place to stay but I was reluctant to stay with them. We later heard he spent jail time & was on drugs!

It rained the whole way to 103 and the road to Uhler looked bad even with chains on so we decided to go up to Eagle, spend the night and try again the next day. The drive was beautiful–mountain roads, a little scary, but the wildflowers were in full bloom-it was 65 miles and we arrived late. Nothing to be had in the way of a room. The scenery was great-the town built on the south shore of the Yukon River. They were rebuilding after huge big flood last year. We were pretty tired by then so we decided to stay at the local campground and try to get some sleep. It was hot and lots of mosquitoes-& we couldn't roll the windows down. After about 15 minutes we decided to leave and drive back to Chicken. We stopped at Summit (an abandoned road house on the Dawson-Fairbanks sled dog trail) and slept about 1 ½ hrs-headed back-luckily it was daylight most of the time.

June 30   Summit-Chicken-Tok

The road to Uhler still looked bad and all of the rivers high. No rooms at Chicken so we headed back to Tok. Met Mike and Cody there. Had breakfast with them and got a room at Tok Motel. We slept about 2 ½ hrs. Ordered a washing machine that Maury forgot to get in Fairbanks and checked email-watched Fox News and fell asleep early.

July 1   Tok-Uhler

The next AM we picked up the washing machine, did some laundry, called home and Barbara. Maury bought some wood 2x4s and loaded them on the truck – I promptly walked into them and got a big goose egg-iced it down-got gas and headed off to Uhler again. Arrived 103 at 3:00 and put on chains. The road was bad but we made it on a wing and a prayer arriving at 5:30. Maury disappeared and I put things away. Thought I would be praised for perseverance but no reward! Got to bed at 11:00.

July 2

Maury got up early, made coffee and finished the expense account. No compensation for mental or physical stress or loss of sleep. Tried our BBQ but couldn't get it to work so I fried our Tok steaks. Spotted a moose across the creek. Got a little gold; ½ oz.

Fourth of July.   Uhler-Chicken

We got our old apartment at Busby's & went to town (the Post Office). It was raining all day so the 4th celebration was pretty wet-the steaks were good and they had games and prizes-the big one being a helicopter trip for part of the next day. My ticket was one digit off! Maury was busy talking to all of the miners about mining methods. We went over to Sue's after the BBQ & met our Uhler guys there. Sue had a combo from Fairbanks and they were pretty good. We finally got up and danced when they played "I Can't Stop Loving You". One lady took our picture and came over to show us the ones she took. She said she was going to show it to her kids back home to show that even old folks could still have fun! Ugh! They even had fireworks-although they weren't too impressive on a blue sky. The guys from Uhler decided to go back although we had an extra bedroom. I was worried about them driving back in the rain but they assured me they would be OK-the road down would be easier on a few drinks. It was surprising to see how many people came out of the woods-a lot more, actually, than you might expect ("Chicken Fest" is growing).

July 5   Chicken-Uhler

We had breakfast at Bronk's (owner of a huge store & RV park). The young couple who were running the restaurant were from Rifle, CO. We returned to camp by noon-the road was pretty bad and we said a few prayers on the way! Grant and Cody were on the mountain cutting down trees to get better Internet reception. Made chili for dinner. Maury went up to the CC to check email. Took the last of my medicine and went to bed at 11:00.

July 6   Uhler

Not much going on. Maury had a busy day and was pretty tired. We both fell asleep watching an old John Wayne movie. Ron came down and had a drink with us. I stayed inside-the mosquitoes were busy!

July 7   Uhler

Filled the camper's water tank again with creek water (for washing, showers & toilet). Aaron got news his wife was starting divorce proceedings. He will leave with Michael next week. Cody leaves today and should return in 3 weeks. Had a talk with Glenn. He said the only money he will make this summer is if Zana pays him to keep Ron here. Maury and Mike off on the Buffalo (amphib/ATV) to check claims. Maury is all upset about email not going thru. Maury informed me that Ron said our RV now belongs to XII Caesars (Ron's company). He's pulling his old tricks again. I guess we'll have words over this. Having trouble with the dump truck. Maury et al went downstream to high bank-no luck! Bronk and his brother, Thor, came for a visit. They are starting a mining museum & looked at Louie's old equipment plus the old Maytag washer. Did my hair today and it looks pretty good. The power off to camper-started generator-fried salmon cakes, potatoes and corn. Watched part of "Slap Shot", a movie-lots of bad language-turned it off. Glenn will take Mike to Fairbanks and see about the pump for the washplant.

July 10

Awoke early found loose wire on battery. A lazy day-am getting in a lot of reading and writing. I'm on my 6th book. Glenn left with Aaron to Fairbanks. All operations stopped until pump repaired. Watched "Oceans 11" and went to bed early.

July 11.   Rained all day. Creek very high. Hope we don't have move to higher ground. Maury brought Ron down for breakfast-fried French toast and bacon. Rain Rain-the creek has changed to a roaring torrent-trees and boulders coming down with current. The Glenn's John Deere excavator on the other side was getting dangerously close to the river as the bank was eating away. After much deliberation, Grant and Jim got in the Marooka and crossed the river-Jim moved the excavator back & they returned to much appreciation from all-Jerry very proud of Grant's part in the procedure. It rained all evening-not possible to get out to main road as planned.

July 13

Lazy day. Maury getting discouraged. The Taylor Highway is closed for repairs-Glenn unable to get back.

July 14

Rained again. Turning cold-turned on generator to recharge batteries. Maury and Grant went up to work on the road (repairing Glenn's "water bars"-diversion ditches) They saw caribou today. I started a pastel of an Eskimo girl. It isn't that good-I'm out of practice-but it keeps me busy. Maury and Grant say the road is now passable.

July 15   Uhler-Boundary-Uhler

Went with Maury to Boundary on the Top of the World Highway in hopes of getting gas. The owner, George, is full of stories (he's known as Crazy George by people in Chicken) about bear and latest stories about miners. No luck getting gas. George was pretty upset about his business (too much rain). On our way back we met Theresa & her father stopped at a barrier waiting for a pilot car (rumors are her father is Chicago Mafia). They were driving around looking for migrating caribou. Reported that road to Chicken a disaster. She was rather vague about what her role was at the Fortymile DOT camp. Maury thinks her husband is on a road crew. We returned to camp around 6:30. The road was bad as usual. Our battery was low and it was pretty cold in the RV.

July 16.

Jerry and Grant went off to Dawson to get gas and water and to check on our battery. Glenn returned and brought our license plate for the camper. The road from Chicken was very bad he came back on a makeshift road. He was stranded in Chicken for 5 days (did some excavator work for Bronk).

July 17

Slept late today. Maury was gone most of the day. I spotted a moose down stream but couldn't get a photo.

July 18

Maury worked today at the wash plant and came in very tired.

July 19   Uhler-Tok

We're going to Tok today-may spend the night-will shop for groceries & do laundry. Met Chris from Baby Creek while waiting for pilot car. Had some good pointers on Skype. Stayed at Tok Motel.

July 20   Tok-Chicken-Tok-Delta-Fairbanks

Bought groceries and headed back to Chicken. Got an email from Ron urgent need for parts-teeth for Glenn's excavator. Couldn't find them in Tok or Delta so went on to Fairbanks. No rooms available-finally found a room at Blue Roof B&B run by Joe Haines. Not too good but better than sleeping in the truck.

July 21   Fairbanks-Tok
    Started looking for parts-called Jim Sullivan-he said we didn't have enough info. Emailed Glenn who emailed back to Jim. Jim said he had them in stock. We had tea with Bruce Foote & his wife-quite a place-we had to wait while they cleared a place for us to sit down. Finally got the parts. Jim's little dog jumped up into my lap while sitting in the truck with the door open waiting for the parts. Quite a feat-46 inches from the ground. Jim called him but he wouldn't budge. Jim finally had to pick him up bodily to get him out of the truck. I guess he wanted to go for a ride. Stayed the night in Tok.

July 22   Tok-Uhler
    Left Tok at 5:00 AM. Left Chicken at 7:05. The road was nearly washed out but we made it thru. We got to 103 at 9:00 AM. Waited till 10:15 & started down the road to camp. Met Jerry, Grant & Jim half way-the road was terrible but we made it.

July 23   Uhler
    Maury worked the gold room & I finished my pastel. We finally got the grill working and had steak and sausage. Sent an email to Duncan back in Woodland Park to check on overcharge from Tok Motel & to order meds from Medco.

July 24
    Maury busy with instructions for gold room. We're getting small nuggets. Glenn is working on road to Ice Hole. Should be mining again in 2 days. Short on fuel again-road closed to Chicken till next week.

July 25.
    Grant and Jim in Boundary to see about gas. Maury busy at gold room. I worked on autobiography and finished pastel. Maybe Maury won't be too tired to watch a movie tonight – no luck – in bed at 8:00.

July 26 – 27
    Nothing to write home about!

July 28.
    Susan's birthday. Feeling blue. Grant, Jerry & Jim to Tok. Got stuck in the mud on the way. Jerry very upset. Watched "Tender Mercies"-I'm on my 15th book.

July 29
    Glenn to Fairbanks w/ pickup-got stuck. All trucks stuck-left 3 pickups at 103. Will try to figure out how to bring gas & diesel to camp.

July 30
    Washed hair-added color-look like a new person. Grant and Jim trying to bring gas to camp.

July 31

Glenn & Cody arrived with Dave. Glenn will work on road again. Has family problems. Cody and David will work wash plant. Jerry's 80th birthday. I baked a cake, did a fruit cobbler and made rice and beans. Went up to CC They had pork chops and fresh corn from CO. Sat around fire got pretty cold.

Aug 2

Both of us grouchy today. Must be getting time to leave. Still running tests (digging test pits). It's been hot.

Aug 3

Maury met a bear this AM. The bear has been visiting our tent and has torn several holes in it. We took hot showers-felt much better!

Aug 4

No word from Medco. Will probably go to Tok tomorrow if we don't hear something. Cody will dredge on Darling Creek (a nearby tributary of Uhler)-looks like a good possibility.

Aug 5   Uhler-Tok

Left for Tok at 7:15 – got an appointment at Tok Clinic-very nice people-they gave me 1-month supply of med. Called Medco and they said my med was on the way. Did our laundry and Cody's. Maury tried to get a part for Glenn's pickup. Had a good dinner at Westmark (a motel with a restaurant)-prime rib!

Aug 7   Tok-Chicken

Stayed at Burnt Paw Motel-great cabin. Left at noon with groceries. Got to Chicken-road closed-washed out again. Stayed in one of Bronk'scabins-2 beds – not much else. Went to Sue's for lunch & put perishables in Bronk's freezer. Met Rose from Eagle and her lady friend stranded when the Taylor Hwy closed. Sue helped them out. Rumor is Rose buys Sue's liqueur stock at end of the season. My meds arrived at post office.

Aug 8   Chicken-Uhler

Breakfast at Busby's. Lou very nice and showed me her Skype telephone that she said worked a lot better than calling via computer. It's got a WIFI connection with the HughesNet router. Called Claire and got her answering machine. Maury did some pay-for-gold panning. Met 3 guys who flew up from Houston, wanted to see Alaska and bought a beat up Subaru they paid $1000 for-said it runs good. They were getting some gold from Bronk's dirt. We suggested they contact Mike Busby for dredging. Met Sue's boyfriend from Fairbanks. He has a routine on Metamucil, "The Staple of Life"-was kind of funny. Sue was all depressed about her business losing money. She said Steve was there on a conjugal visit! Finally got away-first car out in convoy-road pretty bad. Road into Uhler not too bad-got back at 5:00 PM. Had another visit from Smokey – another hole in tent.

Aug 9
Cleaned house-checked meds-packed one Priority Box to send. Read somewhere that the secret to keeping young is finding the age you want and sticking to it.

Aug 10
Talked to Glenn about getting the RV out-offered him $1000. He says he can't do it for any price. Cleaned fridge and took stock of food. Maury went to Chicken for fuel-left at 1:15-returned at 9:15. Went up to the CC to check gold.

Aug 11 & 12
All's quiet on the northern front.

Aug 13
Baked a chocolate cake-pretty good but lopsided due to RV not level. Ate some and sent the rest up to the CC.

Aug 14   Uhler-Chicken
Back to Chicken for fuel and coffee. They ran out at the CC. Left at noon and were ready to return at 3:00 but the DOT wouldn't let us thru. Spent the night at Bronk's no top sheets! Hot.

Aug 15   Chicken-Uhler
Left at 8:00 in convoy. Arrived Uhler at noon. Cody put the bumper guards on RV which had been removed for the trip in from highway. We will leave Aug 23 when we all go to Tok and Cody goes back to CO.

Aug 18   Uhler
Nothing unusual. Rain, lightning and thunder. Made biscuits. Watched first tape of Dr Quinn Med Women.

Aug 19
Getting things together to leave.

Aug 20
Looks like Cody will get to keep the gold nugget he took out of Uhler on his last trip home. He may be the only recipient of gold. Ron is obsessed with looking at his gold thru a microscope. Maury thinks he has all the 50 or so largest nuggets named! When they go to Chicken they will get Bronk to evaluate Cody's nugget. If Cody doesn't get it, I suppose Ron will add it to last year's gold and put it in his drawer so he can look at it often!

Aug 23
Cody helped Maury winterize the RV.

Aug 24   Uhler-Tok

Up early and ready to go at 8:30. All will go to Tok-everyone except us will go to Fairbanks and we will head out for CO-not what was planned originally. Some of us were to go to Walker Fork to do assessment work-don't know what happened to that idea (Ron's original investment in Alaska was for 30 or more claims on Walker Fork. After Louie died the Uhler claims came on the market & Ron bought an option on them). Maury was to be paid big money on paper based on his last earnings in the oil patch. I even got the job of cook-on paper. Got the truck serviced & stayed at the Burnt Paw.

Aug 25   Tok-Woodland Park

Headed home. Made it to Whitehorse and stayed at the Best Western Gold Rush Inn. We had dinner in their restaurant and stayed awhile to listen to live music. We were checking the truck and a couple came by & suggested we put everything inside the truck as there was a lot of drug crime going on. So we packed all we could inside and went back to the hotel.

The next night we made it to Fort Nelson and stayed at an old hotel there. Three more nights on the road – great scenery – last stop in Wheatland, WY, and were back in WP by noon on day 6, Aug 31, 2010. A long journey-we were pretty glad to be home but not looking forward to the mountain of mail awaiting us.

One added note: I was glad to get Maury's beard shaved off. He was beginning to look like Santa Claus.

Mileages:

WP-Chicken	3120
WP-Dawson	3010
Chicken-MP103	37
Dawson-MP103	88
Chicken-Tok	78
Tok-Anchorage	318
Tok-Delta	97
Tok-Fairbanks	202

SUMMER 2011

June 16   WP-Eden

After much preparation especially Maury's weeks of research and work on the solar system he intends to install at the gold camp we finally got packed up and ready to head off to Alaska. Our friends, Danny and Jennifer Alfrey, came over and helped us fold up the pop-up camper that we were taking. After the camper was ready and the pickup loaded with "stuff" including the solar panels, etc., etc., etc., we headed off with Duncan and Carol for our first stop in Eden, Utah, for Sean and Whitney's wedding. We got away around noon and spent the night in Grand Junction then on to Eden arriving the 17th. After an hour or so of confusion about our reservations, we finally settled in at Wolf Creek Resort, a very nice 3-BR condo. That night was a very nice outdoor party for the couple and each gave a really nice talk to all of us thanking everyone for coming.

Saturday, June 18   Eden

The wedding was held in the Beck's (Whitney's parents-Lou & Cynthia) backyard-a beautiful setting-yellow daisies and wild flowers in full bloom. A white trellis covered with sun flowers was the altar and the day was perfect. A true Garden of Eden ceremony.

Father's Day June 19 We left Eden for Alaska-not a happy day since Karen called and said Dad was in the hospital but doing OK.

June 20 Stopped in Butte, MT, and bought a bear fence and bear spray.

On to Fort McCloud and stayed at the Daisy Mae campground. After a night in Valleyview, we drove to Muncho Lake arriving June 22. On the way we saw more wildlife than ever before including buffalo, bear and mountain goats. We camped near the lake-a very nice picnic spot-the lake a beautiful blue-green and a very nice lodge, The Northern Rockies Lodge, run by Germans. We went in for a drink but didn't find anything tempting on the menu.

June 23 Roads getting dusty where repairs were being made. Had a flat on the camper south of Teslin Lake. Found the spare flat too. Were about to take the bad tires to Whitehorse when a couple stopped with a battery driven air compressor which inflated the spare. They're retired military and live in North Pole near Fairbanks. Limped into Whitehorse, stayed overnight and bought 2 new tires for the camper.

June 24
Worst road during trip was between Burwash and Alaska where the road is not maintained because of a screwy treaty between US and Canada. Made it to Tok.

June 25   Tok Uhler
Had a nice surprise at the campground in Tok discovering they had a trio; guitar, banjo and violin. Bought supplies and some apple fritters (the best this side of Houston & Lampassas) and took off for Chicken. Saw Sue Wiren, our favorite Chickenite, and got a boisterous welcome from the Busbys, left the camper at Milepost 103 and arrived in camp at 7:00 PM. Found everything working in our big camper except for a few "problems" left behind by folks who stayed in it earlier. Worked on the water supply pumped up from the creek.

June 26-27   Uhler
Rained all day-cleaned RV and put supplies away.

June 28   Uhler-Tok-Uhler
Back to TOK-took Scott with us to get a pickup left for repairs. Called Karen-Dad not doing well-Dr suggests hospice. Doesn't look like Dad will recover-not a good day. Went back to camp-decided to go to Florida.

July 1   Tok-Fairbanks
Back to Tok with camper-Bronk's dad, Spike, helped us with reservations. Drove to Fairbanks and stayed there until my flight at 6:00 AM. Maury will leave camper in Tok for a few repairs-repairman said we can keep it there.

July 2   Fairbanks-Orlando
Off to Orlando-will arrive there at 11:00 PM. Very confusing-changed planes in Seattle and Dallas-got lost once.

July 3   Orlando
Dad sleeping most of the time- thought I was Grandma and he was already in heaven.

July 4
Karen drops me off in the AM before work-Dad sleeping most of the time. Hospice nurse on duty 24 hours.

July 5
Dad woke up and asked for coffee-I told him Maury said hello and he asked where he was-I said Alaska. He just rolled his eyes.

July 6
Not a good day-everyone in the facility watching the CaseyAnthony trial. Dad's eyes shut most of the time.

July 7

Thunder, lightening and rain. Barbara, Nelson and Aislinn arrive and help pack up Dad's things. Karen arrives after work-Dad passes on with eyes wide open-the end has finally come-

July 8

Cleaned room of all Dad's things and called family.

July 11

Karen and I went to the funeral home to finalize arrangements. Dad's funeral policy for cremation and expenses covered all but $10.00. He saved $1,200 on his final day. That would have made him happy.

July 12-13

Went through albums and all the things stored at Karen's. Barb took all to Good Will. Closed safe deposit box.

July 14-15

Went down to the nursing home to thank all of the nurses and administrators. Made arrangements to sell his birthday chair.

July 16   Orlando-Fairbanks

Back to Alaska-arrive 12:00 midnight Alaska time. Maury was there to meet me-had the camper set up at River's Edge Campground.

July 16   Fairbanks-Denali

Drove with camper to Denali Park and took a day's tour. Saw grizzly bears, caribou and lots of mountain goats. Also visited Jeff King's sled dog facility.

July 19   Denali-Uhler

Left Denali at 8:30 AM and drove to gold camp arriving at 10 PM. Camp road bad because of rain-put chains on-Glenn and Scott came out to meet us.

July 20   Uhler

Cleaned camper and put things away.

Jul7 21

Wrote to Cara. Glenn left in disgust-will he return?

July 22

Hot today-things pretty much shut down-to bed early.

July 23

A big bear knocked on Jim's door.

July 24

Got news of Zana's (Ron's wife) accident-fell down at home near Basalt while watering flowers-she will need help. Glenn returned-he fixed strawberry margaritas. Guess he will stay on if things improve. He saw Casey at his mine and says he's doing well. (Casey & Tim left last year. Casey took his inheritance & bought some claims north of Fairbanks-now has them listed for $6.5 million) Glenn also had lunch with Judd Edgerton, a neighboring miner.

July 25

Maury finished the solar panels and hooked them up. Heard a bear under my window-heavy breathing-thought it was Maury at first!

July 26

Weather good-built a fire pit in front of camper. Sat outside, cooked steak, and listened to music. Harry came with 7 oz gold from his claim on Walker Fork that Ron sold him. Harry used our shaker table to separate gold from concentrates. He's doing better than we are.

July 27

Glenn left for Tok-not happy.

July 28

Planted Sean and Whitney's daisy seeds. Woke up at 3:00 AM with sore neck. Bed early.

July 29

Maury gone all day. Baked a cake-turned out pretty good! Grant & Scott to Tok.

July 30

Washed my hair in camper shower. Maury and Glenn talked over margaritas. Played gin rummy with Maury-I lost several games-bed early.

August 1

Baked German chocolate cake for Jerry's birthday. Ate dinner at cabin (CC).

August 2

Found some gold today. Ron all excited about Egyptian Pyramid-best yet (Ron has rather weird names for all his test pits).

August 3

Sunny today. Glenn delivered margaritas.

August 4

Rain and chilly. Will go Valdez tomorrow.

August 5   Uhler-Valdez ("vawl.deez")

Off to Valdez-picked up camper in Tok and made it to Valdez at 8:30 PM. Scenery beautiful, mountains and high waterfalls-much different from our part of Alaska.

August 6   Valdez

Went to two very nice museums-drove though town-harbor surrounded by mountains. Stopped at Pipeline Bar- saw floor show with can-can girls. Maury bought a garter and got to remove it from the leg of can-can girl-hmmm. Arranged for a silver salmon fishing trip.

August 7

Met Dave, the Captain, at the dock at 7:30 AM-rained most of the day-caught 10 salmon-I got the big one. Arranged to send most to Woodland Park-called Duncan and alerted him.

August 8   Valdez-Big Lake

Had to put camper down in rain. Made it to Wasilla near Big Lake. Met Cynthia, Whitney's mother, and followed her home (Lou piloting commercial flights to China). She cooked some of our salmon-had a nice visit-spent the night-left early AM. They have a float plane-it's a beautiful place.

August 9   Big Lake-Tok

Arrived Tok at 4:00 PM-rain again-spent the night there. Left the camper to have air conditioner removed (rain leaking through it) and replaced with a vent.

August 10   Tok-Uhler

Went by clinic to check neck pain. Doctor diagnosed spasm. Arrived camp at 3:00 PM. Prepared poached salmon for dinner.

August 11

Slept well-used hot pads on my neck. Chili for dinner. Ron planning my demise. He asked Maury if he would come back next year if it wasn't for me. I guess I'm a pain in the neck.

August 12

More gold today. Made chicken noodle soup. Bed early. Maury getting expert at gin rummy.

August 13

Black bear came around the camper. Maury shot his pistol to scare him off. A helicopter landed and a Milrock geologist said he had shot and wounded a grizzly upstream. Our black bear is getting too familiar in camp.

August 14

Bears were back. Maury met one nose-to-nose this AM staring at each other through the back window of the camper. He/she had torn off duct tape covering busted tail light on RV.

Maybe we need that bear fence. Maury and Ron went upstream. We talked to Glenn about getting camper out-impossible?

August 15
Crew all went to Chicken for supplies. Rained all day.

August 16
No work till noon. Got boxes ready to send home. Bear looked in our window at noon while we ate lunch-he's pretty big.

August 17
Two weeks to go! Maury had a long conversation with Ron about Glenn. Maury not happy about the way things are going. Ron said Maury was free to go.

August 18   Uhler-Chicken-Uhler
We planned to go to Fairbanks to ship guns home. Went into Chicken and sold guns to Bronk. Returned to camp and Maury decided to leave immediately. Maury gave Ron his felt hat that Ron had been coveting and Ron bought our camper and solar system. Packed up all personal effects-what a job!

August 19   Uhler-Dawson, YT
Left camp for Dawson via Top of the World Highway. All roads in bad condition. We were covered in mud when we arrived in Dawson. Had a flat on camper east of Canadian border. Arrived Dawson at 3:00 PM-bought tire and rim- had lunch and went on. Stopped around 5:00 at Klondike River Lodge-slept well!

August 22   Teslin Lake, YT
Stayed there in a very nice campground by the lake. Met a man from Newfoundland who gave me a coin from there.

August 23   Muncho Lake, BC
Saw 6 moose hunters loading up their gear into a float plane for a flight into the back country.

August 24   Dawson Creek, BC

August 25   Banff, AB
Couldn't find a camping spot in Jasper - had breakfast in lodge at Lake Louise-beautiful as ever. Stayed in the last campground in Banff.

August 26   Shelby, MT
Engine overheating on passes-went through Yellowstone Park-used JB weld to patch crack in coolant reservoir while waiting for engine to cool in Sylvan Pass.

August 28   Cody, WY
Spent 2 nights-had lunch with the Fowlers, went to a show and saw Esther Johanssen (Maury's old nursemaid-in her 90s & daughter of cook for Maury's grandparents at Trout Creek Ranch).

August 29   Dutch John, UT
Called the Buzardes-spent the night with them. Buzz recovering from bad health experience. Helped him in successful experiment in sampling scotch.

August 31   Frisco, CO
Spent night at The Summit Inn-got coolant reservoir replaced.

Sept 1   Woodland Park
Arrived home at last!